RUNES

RUNES
HOW TO READ THEM

RACHEL NEWCOMBE

This pocket edition first published in 2025

First published in hardback as *Runes Illustrated* in 2023

Amber Books Ltd
United House
North Road
London N7 9DP
United Kingdom
www.amberbooks.co.uk
Facebook: amberbooks
YouTube: amberbooksltd
Instagram: amberbooksltd
X(Twitter): @amberbooks

Copyright © 2025 Amber Books Ltd

All rights reserved. No part of this work may be reproduced, stored in a retrieval system, or transmitted in any form or by any means, electronic, mechanical, photocopying, recording, or otherwise, without the prior permission of the copyright holder.

ISBN: 978-1-83886-586-3

Printed in China

Design & Editorial: Amber Books Ltd

CONTENTS

6
FOREWORD

8
HOW TO USE THE RUNES

62
THE RUNIC ALPHABET

126
ANCIENT RUNESTONES

220
INDEX

224
PICTURE CREDITS

FOREWORD

Welcome to the world of runes and ancient runestones.

The mystery and nature of the runes have fascinated people for centuries. Perhaps known best as simple carved images on stone or wood, runic symbols have several purposes. For ancient communities they were one of the main forms of written communication and served as an alphabet. However, the carved symbols also held symbolic meanings and were used for divination purposes.

In this book you'll discover more about both of these elements. Part 1 offers an introduction on how to use runes, taking you through everything from choosing a set of runes and getting to know your stones, to using them for divination and traditional rune casting and learning specific rune casting layouts.

Part 2 explores the meaning and significance of each of the runic symbols in the Elder Futhark and helps readers to understand the symbolism that may appear in runic layouts. Two other runic alphabets are also mentioned, namely the Anglo-Saxon Futhorc and the Younger or Scandinavian Futhark, however, the main focus is on the more popular Elder Futhark runes.

Part 3 focuses on the runic inscriptions of historic ancient runestones that have been discovered over the years. It offers a virtual tour around Scandinavia, exploring some of the most famous and historically significant runestones, as well as looking at runestones found in the British Isles. In addition to the stones themselves, there's also discussion of some of the significant items that have been discovered with runic inscriptions carved on them.

Not surprisingly, there have been many different name interpretations applied to runes over the years. Therefore, at the end of the book, you'll find a helpful guide to the alternative names that are often given to the runes in the Elder Futhark.

Enjoy your runic journey!

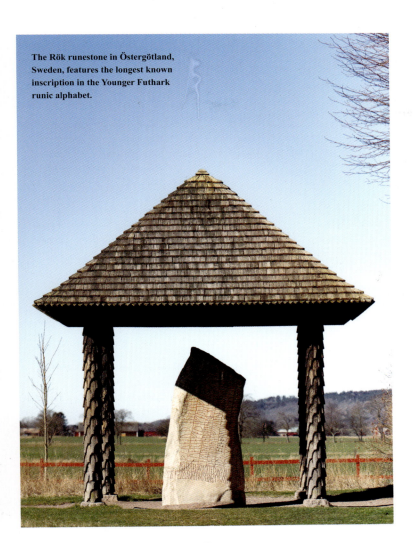

The Rök runestone in Östergötland, Sweden, features the longest known inscription in the Younger Futhark runic alphabet.

HOW TO USE THE RUNES

Opposite: Round carved wooden runes in an open traditional cloth storage bag.

What are Runes?
Runes are ancient angular symbols that are typically carved into stone, wood and metal. The word 'rune' aptly means mystery, secret or whisper. It's likely to stem from the early Germanic word, 'ru' and Norse word, 'rún', which both mean 'mystery'.

Each rune has a phonetic sound and a symbolic meaning and, when combined and used as a form of alphabet, were frequently used to create runic inscriptions. For example, ancient runic inscriptions have been found carved on burial stones and objects such as swords, pottery and jewellery.

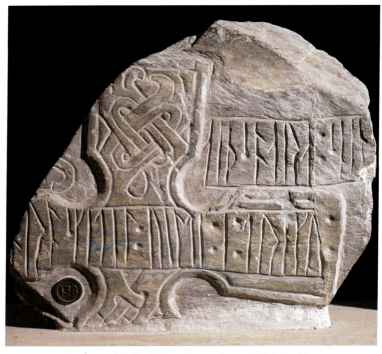

A fragment of the Roskitil runic cross found at Kirk Braddan, Isle of Man, England.

In addition, runes have traditionally been used as an ancient form of divination or oracle system to gain insight into problems and situations. It's believed that each symbol has its own energy and meaning, and alongside the use of personal intuition, could be used to help figure out potential solutions. Ancient civilizations in countries such as Norway, Sweden, Finland, Denmark,

Germany and the British Isles all used runes as a form of communication, meaning and symbolic importance, and they may have played a part in culture in other parts of the world too. Exactly how the runic alphabet developed is unclear, but it may stem from the Phoenician alphabet.

Runic symbols dating back to the Bronze Age have been discovered by archaeologists. One of the earliest known mentions of runes as a divination method is by the Roman writer Tacitus, in his book *Germania*. Written about AD 98, it describes how runic divination was practised in times of trouble or confusion. As an alphabet, runes were gradually replaced by the emergence of Latin, but were still often used in Scandinavian cultures until the 20th century as a form of carved decorative symbol. And, of course, runic divination has retained its popularity in some quarters and is still performed by many people today.

Various different alphabets are used on runes and, like other forms of communication, they have been adapted over the years. One of the oldest and most well-known forms is the Germanic runic alphabet called the Elder Futhark, which consists of 24 runes.

As people in Northern Europe gradually travelled and settled in different countries, the runic alphabet evolved to meet their linguistic and communicative needs. The Elder Futhark developed into the Younger or Scandinavian Futhark in about AD 750, or around the beginning of the Viking age.

In turn, the Anglo-Saxon or Old English Futhorc subsequently developed in England, where an additional nine symbolic runes were added to bring the alphabet up to 33.

Knowledge about runes has been passed down through Germanic folklore and ancient Nordic tales, mythology and legends. According to Norse mythology, for example, runes have existed since time began and many stories involving the Norse god Odin feature them. Archaeological digs and finds have also helped create a greater understanding of runes and the importance that runic inscriptions played in communication, symbolism and personal identity. Runes have been found carved on many items, some of which have been successfully translated while others remain a mystery.

Round wooden runes with pyrographic etched symbols.

Runestones can be made from a variety of materials, including wood, resin, stone and glass.

Runes also feature in modern writings. For example, J. R. R. Tolkien used an adapted runic alphabet in the classic fantasy novel, *The Hobbit*.

How Can Runes be Used?
One of the ways in which runes can be used is as a form of oracle or divination method. Contrary to some opinions, reading runes isn't a form of fortune-telling and won't provide you with exact answers or specific advice. However, runes can offer hints and guidance and suggest different variables that you may want to consider in more detail.

The idea is that as you sit and ask a question or think about issues that are on your mind, your conscious and unconscious minds become focused. When you cast the runes, the stones that emerge are choices made by your subconscious, or a mirror of your subconscious mind. They reflect what you already know deep down, but may have been hiding from your conscious mind due to fear, worry or uncertainty.

Keeping a note of runic readings can be helpful when you're learning to master the runes.

The emergence of the rune symbols gives you the chance to work through your questions with clarity, intuition and deeper understanding.

It's important to embrace your powers of intuition when reading the runes, as that will help you to delve into the nitty-gritty, work out the details and come to any conclusions. Reading and understanding the runes can help you both with self-reflection and self-discovery.

Remember that it's important to avoid using the runes too much, or as a crutch that you go straight to the moment you have any burning worries. They won't be helpful in every circumstance and you may weaken your intuitive abilities if you overuse divination. Instead, you'd be wise to save your readings for questions and queries that you can't immediately find answers for or situations where you need a deeper level of guidance.

It's not only readings that you can use runes for. Traditionally runes were used as a form of written alphabet. As you explore the nature of runes and get to know the symbols, you may feel the need to try runic writing too. It can help deepen your connection with runes, as well as aid your familiarization with the use of particular symbols.

A set of 24 square wooden runes featuring the Elder Futhark runes, plus one blank rune known as the Wyrd stone.

Hand-carved and polished wooden runes.

You could start by choosing a single rune that you feel drawn to and try writing or carving it. For example, you could write the rune and put it in a place where you'll see it regularly, such as pinned on a noticeboard or on your desk. Or you could draw the symbol on the front of a notebook, etch it on a piece of wood or stitch it onto your rune storage bag.

If there are several runes that you feel drawn to, you could create a written combination of runes, like the inscriptions found on ancient runestones. It's not the easiest form of alphabet to write with because it doesn't contain the same letters as the alphabet as we know it today, but you could use the meanings or sounds of the runes to create phrases that feel meaningful to you.

If there's a particular rune that you are attracted to, it could become your personal power symbol – a symbol that you strongly connect with. Some people use power symbols as talismans (see page 39) and carve them on pieces of jewellery to wear as pendants or earrings.

Choosing a Set of Runes

If you're going to be reading runes regularly, you'll need to own a set. Ready-made sets of runes can be found in specialist gift shops and bookstores or purchased online. Some rune sets come with a basic guide to reading them, whereas others simply provide the runes themselves. The choice of set is very much a personal decision. It's important to choose the runes that feel right for you, especially if you want to get the most out of using and reading them.

Runes can be made from a variety of materials, such as wood, stone, glass, clay,

**A complete set of Elder Futhark runes laid out
in a circle for easy reference.**

A set of runes made from carved white stone.

metal, gemstone, bone, ceramic or crystal, with the runic symbols carved or inscribed on them. Different materials appeal to different people but, if unsure of which you'd prefer, it's helpful to hold a few different runes to see which feel more 'you'.

For example, you might prefer the natural hand-carved feeling of wooden runes in your hand, or the cold polished sensation of runes made from glass. Or it might be the case that you feel a particular resonance to a specific type of material. For example, you may feel that a certain type of wood, such as oak, birch or ash, carries

Small polished tumbled gemstones, such as rose quartz, are a popular material for runes.

importance for you and helps you feel more connected to the earth. Rune sets made from natural gemstones are popular and you can choose sets based on the properties of the gemstones. For example, amethyst crystals are said to help intuition, whereas hematite can be grounding and protecting.

There's no right or wrong choice, so go for whichever rune material feels most tactile, comforting, magical or practical for you to use.

It's also important that you choose runes that are clear to read, so make sure that you're easily able to distinguish each of the symbols. You don't want to get confused between different runic symbols or find that the symbol begins to wear off over time. The size of runes is likely to differ depending on the material they're made of – some gemstone runes can be quite small – so make sure the size doesn't affect your ability to read them.

Runes can be different shapes too, such as flat, round or symmetrical. Think about how you plan to use your runes, as this could affect which shape is best for you. For example, rounded runes might be fine for doing single rune readings, but if you plan to do rune layouts, it's more practical to have flat runes.

Regular practice is the best way to get to grips with runic divination.

Image of The Three Norns, from Norse mythology, painted by J. I. Lund in 1844.

The quality of runes varies and it's worth investing in a good, well-made set that will last, rather than a cheap version that will disintegrate quickly. Look for reviews of rune sets or retailers, to get an idea of the quality and durability of the runes. If you have a limited budget, or aren't sure if rune reading is for you, then it's fine to choose a basic set to get started with. You can always upgrade to more personalized runes in the future.

If you can't find a set of runes that you like, or you've been using a bought set for a while and want to upgrade, you could try making your own (see page 42). The process of making your own runes is a ritual in itself and one that could help you connect to the history of the divination method, as you'll be handcrafting runes in the traditional way.

Two runes belonging to a set made from natural stone.

Five runes surrounding a blank Wyrd stone.

Getting to Know Your Runes

Once you've acquired a set of runes, it's time to get to know them. If you've purchased a set of Elder Futhark runes – the ones most commonly used – you'll have a set of 24 runes. Some sets will also contain an extra runestone, left blank. This is known as the Wyrd stone – it gets its name from the Norns, the three goddesses of fate in Norse mythology, which were collectively called Wyrd.

However, it is worth noting that you might also come across references to the blank rune being described as Odin's Rune, after one of the principal gods in Norse mythology. But, do not confuse this with the traditional single rune cast, which is also often referred to as Odin's Rune. Whether you choose to include the Wyrd stone in your readings or not is a matter of personal choice.

As a complete beginner, it's understandable if you feel daunted about using your runes. Before you plunge straight into attempting a rune reading, it's a good idea to spend some time acquainting yourself with each of the stones first. You can do this in several ways.

A rune reader holding and studying the Berkana rune, which means 'birch' and symbolizes new beginnings.

First, you could aim to take it slowly and acquaint yourself with one rune a day. If you have your runes stored in a bag, make time each day to sit quietly and blind pick one rune from your bag. With each rune you choose, get to know the runic symbol and read up on what it represents. If you pick the same one twice, discard it and go again. Learning one rune at a time can be a gentle and less stressful way of getting to know your runes.

Alternatively, if you've got more time and are keen to progress, lay out all the runes in your set and go through them one by one. Study the design and style of the symbols and read up on the details of each individual rune.

Some people like to build up a connection with their runes and their higher self, so that they feel more in tune with their energies. You could try meditating while holding your runes or use mindfulness techniques.

For example, spend some time being quiet and still and hold the runes in your hand. Think about what the texture of the runes feels like against your skin and how each rune makes you feel. Does a particular rune conjure up a certain feeling or emotion, or do you sense a stronger connection to one stone more than others?

Runes were traditionally kept in a small pouch or bag, such as a drawstring bag. Bags made of materials such as silk, velvet or cotton are all suitable. Some people choose black bags, as it's a grounding and protecting colour. As you go about your daily life, you may like to keep your bag of runes near you for a while, for example in your pocket, so that your energies and those of the runes can begin to align.

Runic Divination

Runic divination is the art of reading the runes. Each of the symbols engraved or painted onto the rune stones is believed to have its own individual meaning and symbolic representation and when it appears in a reading, it's there for a reason.

In the Elder Futhark, the set of 24 runes is divided into three aetts, each containing eight stones. Each of the aetts contains a family of runestones, with meanings and messages that are related. Put together, the three aetts offer insight into all the key issues, milestones, obstacles and situations you're likely to encounter in life. Even though they were created thousands of years ago, and are subject to some degree of interpretation, the messages are still relevant today.

By laying out or casting the runes and asking pertinent questions, you could gain insight and understanding to help you navigate your way through life's ups and downs and uncertainties, when making your own choices and decisions.

In fact, to read runes successfully, one of the most important things you need to acknowledge is that the future is never fixed and that you have the power to follow your own path and make your own decisions.

This is based on ancient Norse traditions, which tell us that nothing in the future is set in stone. Instead, the ancient Norse people believed very sensibly that it constantly shifts and is affected by everything happening in the present. If you're on one path, you don't have to remain there if the signs are pointing you in another direction. You possess the strength and power to walk whichever way you feel is right. Learning the art of runic divination takes time, but the more your practise, the more natural it will become.

In order to get the most out of practising runic divination, it's important to carefully choose a time and place to do a reading. You need peace and quiet, away from distractions (whether it be noisy people, music, TV or a busy road) and a spot where you feel comfortable.

Some people like to create a special atmosphere for doing a reading, such as by lighting candles or burning incense, but there's no right or wrong way to go about it. Ideally, you'll need a dedicated cloth for a runic reading, but if you don't have one, make sure you at least have a flat surface free from clutter.

Traditionally a rune cloth is square, plain and made of white material. It needs to be big enough to accommodate the size of your runes, while providing space around them, and should'nt have a distracting pattern on it.

The key issue with any reading of the runes is that your reading area and vision is free from distractions, so that you can be calm, centre your mind, have clarity and concentrate exclusively on the runes. Be prepared to unleash the power of your subconscious and use your intuition to interpret the messages in the stones.

Formulating Questions to Use with Runes

To get the most from a rune reading, it's important to ask the right questions. Unlike divination methods such as pendulum reading, runes don't work well with answering simple 'yes' or 'no' questions, especially as there are no specific rune symbols that mean 'yes' or 'no'. Sometimes people look at the way the rune falls to signify 'yes' or 'no' – for example, an upright rune is taken to mean 'yes' and a reversed rune as 'no' – but this isn't ideal and can result in an unclear reading.

Instead, phrase your questions carefully so that you get better results. For example, rather than asking, 'Will I get a new job?', ask, 'How can I best go about getting a new job?'. Or rather than asking, 'Should I go on holiday?', phrase your question as, 'What benefits could I gain from going on holiday?'.

A set of runes made from carved white stone.

It can be useful to keep your questions broad and open-ended. It's also worth seeking general advice, rather than an answer to a set question. For example, you could ask, 'What would it be useful for me to know now that could be helpful for me in the future?'. You can speak your question out loud, or simply think about it in your mind.

It's also wise not to ask too many questions at once. More questions don't result in better results, so focus on one question you're seeking answers to. You can always ask another question the next time you do a reading.

In terms of subject matter, there are no rules as to what you can and cannot ask. Some of the common issues typically asked about in rune readings address work, friendships, relationships, love, health, family and careers.

When you're asking your question, be positive and open to the answers the runes provide. Focusing your mind is really important for any rune reading. When you cast the stones, your powers of intuition and your subconscious mind can get to work with analyzing the symbols and working out how they could relate to you and your question. The runes can't be used to think for you and automatically provide you with all the answers, but they can be used to help you think for yourself.

The symbols that the runes reveal are regarded as being a mirror of your subconscious mind. Although you may be unaware of it, you may already have had the answers deep within yourself. Casting the runes and honestly analyzing the symbolism can help bring the solutions to your conscious mind.

The more positive energy you have when you're asking questions and reading the runes, the more likely it is that you'll gain something beneficial from a reading. If you go into it feeling negative, your judgement could be clouded or you may fail to pick up on potential meanings.

How to Read Runes

Learning the art of how to read and understand the messages in the runes is something that takes time, patience and perseverance. Part 2 of the book contains details about each of the runes in the runic alphabet as well as their meaning and significance, which will help you as you decode the messages in the stones.

When you're reading runes, keep an open mind, don't worry or stress about getting it right and treat it as a learning curve. Take time to ponder potential meanings, but don't panic if you're not immediately sure what something means, as it may become clearer at a later stage.

There are various approaches to dealing with runes that land symbol-side down. Some schools of thought say to simply ignore them, whereas others suggest the meanings could relate to issues on the periphery of your life. It is up to individual choice as to whether you read them or not, but for beginners it can be easier to simply discount them.

The same is true for runes that land with the symbol upside down. Some people read these as reversed runes, with a slightly different meaning, but when you're starting out it's more straightforward to stick to one meaning for every symbol, reversed or not.

It's useful to keep a record of your readings and interpretations, either in a rune journal or simply as notes on your mobile phone. For example, you could either note down or take a photo of the runes that appear in the cast, and then record your thoughts. Some meanings that may have been confusing initially may make more sense when you look back at them later. Having a record of your rune readings can help improve your confidence and the accuracy of future readings.

If runes appear that you're not expecting, or seem out of context with your questions, don't dismiss them out of hand. Make a note of the runes and refer back

Small round wooden runes produced from tree branches.

A set of flat hexagonal-shaped wooden runes.

to them at a later stage, as the meanings may become clearer over time. Or it may be that the runes have answers to questions that you've not consciously asked yet.

Over time you may notice the same runes appear frequently in your rune casts. It may simply be a coincidence, but it could also be that those runes are asking you to pay particular attention to them, or that you're being guided to look at their meanings in a deeper manner.

It's not unusual for combinations of certain runes to keep appearing too. Although each individual rune has its own meaning, if they keep coming up alongside other runes, it may be a sign and the meanings can be amplified to give an additional layer to a reading. For example, the runic symbol Raido is associated with journeys and travel and the symbol Wunjo with romance, happiness and fun. If Raido and Wunjo keep appearing together, it may be a message that embarking on a journey could bring increased happiness and perhaps even romance.

Likewise, the rune Fehu is associated with good fortune or prosperity and Gebo can signify a gift or contract. If Fehu and Gebo keep appearing together, they may signify that a new contract – be it work, relationship or friendship related – could bring increased prosperity into your life.

Many Elder Futhark sets now include a blank rune. Known as the Wyrd stone, this rune is set to represent fate or destiny. If it appears in a reading, it may indicate that there's something you're not meant to know yet.

Traditional Rune Casting
One of the oldest ways of reading runes is through a traditional rune casting. Traditional methods have been passed down through different generations over the centuries. One of the oldest known sources is the book *Germania*, by the Roman historian and writer Tacitus.

Written in the 1st century AD, it outlines the runic divination methods of the Germanic people. Although the exact method he describes, which involves cutting a branch from a nut-bearing tree, slicing it into strips and marking each strip with a symbol, isn't entirely practical today, other elements of the rune casting method are still useful.

For example, Tacitus describes how the strips are thrown randomly onto a white cloth, with the person doing the reading looking up at the sky while picking up three strips. They then read the meaning of each symbol one by one.

The traditional rune casting method of randomly throwing the runes onto a cloth in this way is still practised by many rune readers today. Although there are plenty of

Lit candles can be used to create atmosphere when reading the runes.

rune layouts available, some people feel it's a more accessible approach for reading runes, as you don't need to worry about laying them out in a particular way. Others feel that it's a method more in tune with the ancients.

If you're keen to try doing a rune casting the traditional way, first find yourself somewhere quiet and uncluttered to do so. Put a white cloth down on a table in front of you, or on the floor if that's more convenient. Then, take a few moments to quiet your mind and centre your spirit.

Choose a question that you'd like to ask and either say it out loud or think about it in your head.

Gently shuffle your bag of runes, for example by giving them a shake, so the runic symbols become randomly mixed up.

Tip the bag so that the runes scatter out onto your cloth, while remembering to look up so that you can't see the symbols that appear.

Reach out and choose three runes at random and read their meanings one by one. As well as looking at each of the runic meanings, if you wish, you can also consider

A statue in Vienna of the Roman historian, Tacitus, author of the book *Germania*.

what they could mean when taken as a group of three or a runic combination. It could be that these three runes have a message to share that's poignant at this point in time. If you want to keep a record of your runes, or are unsure of any meanings, make a note of them in your runic journal.

When you've finished, collect up all your runes and put them back in your storage bag. Fold up your reading cloth and store all your items safely, ready to use again another time.

Rune Casting Layouts

Compared to traditional rune casting methods, layouts or spreads as they're sometimes known, are regarded as a more modern approach to reading runes – even though some elements of layouts do stem from ancient practices.

Rune casting layouts can provide a more structured approach to reading runes and are often favoured by beginners. They provide you with a basic structure to follow, guidance on how runes should be placed and the order in which they should be read. The layouts share similarities with those used in other divination methods, such as Tarot reading.

For beginners, using a rune casting layout can help considerably when you're trying to work out the messages in the runes. In order to understand and interpret runes to the best of your ability, it helps to know what aspect of a question the runes might be referring to.

In a simple three rune layout, for example, each of the three runes are taken as referring to the past, present and future.

There are numerous different layouts you can use to provide you with flexibility and variety when you're reading. You can choose a layout by personal preference or you may find over time that certain layouts are more suitable to use for answering certain types of questions.

For example, you may find a simple question is better answered with a smaller rune layout, whereas a more complex question may be better contemplated with a bigger layout involving more runes.

When you're starting out you may want to stick to just using a few rune casting layouts, or you may be keen to try out all of them. Whatever your preference, there's no right or wrong way and you can use as many or as few layouts as you feel comfortable with.

Over time you may even begin to develop your own rune cast layouts, which is also equally acceptable. As an oracle method that encourages the use of intuition, it seems only natural to be guided by your intuition as to what new layout could work for your readings.

THE SINGLE RUNE CAST

As the name suggests, the single rune cast – sometimes called Odin's Rune – involves drawing and interpreting one single rune. It's a good place to start for beginners, as it doesn't involve the need to draw multiple runes that need to be placed in specific positions, and instead provides you with just the one rune to analyze. It's also a good choice of rune cast if you have a simple question you'd like to ask or if you're looking for a quick cast to do on a daily basis, such as first thing in the morning or before you go to bed at night.

To carry out a single rune cast, first find yourself a quiet spot to sit with a table or flat surface in front of you, then spend a few moments quietening and focusing your mind. Ideally, try to get rid of any inner chatter going on in your head, as this helps provide you with more clarity and focus for conducting the reading.

Hold your bag of runes in your hand and think about the particular question you're seeking insight into. Gently shake the runes in the bag to muddle them up.

When you feel ready, open up the bag, put your hand in and pick one rune. You can choose completely at random; pick a rune that feels most tactile in your hand or choose the one that feels like it's drawing your energy towards it.

Remove the rune from the storage bag and place it down on the surface in front of you, with its symbol facing upwards. Which runic symbol have you

Raidō, meaning 'ride' or 'journey'.

drawn? Now, it's time to consider the rune you've cast and think about what possible outcomes or answers it could be indicating. Consider it with an open mind and use your intuition.

One useful way in which you could use the single rune cast is to make it a habit to pick a rune first thing in the morning, while asking a simple question such as, 'What do I need to learn today?' or, 'How is my day going to go?'. Think about what the stone could be telling you and jot down details of the runic symbol and your interpretation in a notebook.

At the end of the day, look back on your notes and consider if and how this meaning related to the day you've had. Do any of the messages in the rune ring true for you? Sometimes they may be obvious, whereas on other occasions the relevance may be unclear. Remember, however, that there can be layers of messages in the runes and sometimes it may be that the significance becomes clearer after you've picked runes every day during the week and looked at the bigger picture.

Getting into a daily rune habit is a good way of getting to know the runes and acquaint yourself with the way in which they can share messages. It's also a really helpful way of building up your own confidence with using runes and is a quick and easy way of incorporating the practice into your daily routine.

Mannaz, meaning 'man'

THE THREE RUNE LAYOUT

The Three Rune Layout is a popular rune cast to do as it can provide a good overview of a situation or question. The three runes drawn represent the past, present and future.

This is sometimes referred to as the Three Norns Cast, after the three goddesses of fate in Norse mythology. Urd, Verdandi and Skuld were guardians of the Well of the Wyrd underneath the Yggdrasil, or World Tree. They are known as the Three Norns, or Nornir and are similar to the Fates that appear in Greek mythology.

The runes are laid out in a row, with the first rune on the left, the second in the middle and the third on the right, and they are read from left to right. The rune in the Place of Urd (1) refers to the past; the rune in the Place of Verdandi (2) represents the present and that in the Place of Skuld (3) refers to the future.

1. The Place of Urd – the past

The rune in position one relates to issues, events or influences in the past that could have relevance for the current situation or the question you've asked.

2. The Place of Verdandi – the present

The rune in position two refers to the present circumstances and current

Mannaz, meaning 'man'

Ansuz, meaning 'ash'

Pertho, meaning 'pawn'

A THREE RUNE CAST.

situations or consequences that have occurred due to the influence of the past. It may also represent current issues that need to be tackled and any choices you may need to make in the near future.

3. The Place of Skuld – the future

The rune in position three can be trickier to interpret, as it relates to the future and events that may or may not happen. It can reveal aspects that are currently unknown and that could occur, depending on the choice and decisions you make. It's important to remember that the future isn't set in stone and your own free will and personal actions can influence it.

Three nordic runes, Wunjo, Eihwaz, and Dagaz. This rune combination symbolizes upcoming positive life changes.

A reader analyzing the runes revealed in a Three Rune Layout.

THE FIVE RUNE LAYOUT

Following the theme of layouts involving odd numbers is the Five Rune Layout. There are several variations of this layout in existence, with both the positioning order of the runes and what they are said to represent differing.

In this version, the five runes build up a good overview of a situation or event and offer insight into challenges you could face and goals you'd like to achieve.

To create the Five Rune Layout, the runes are laid out on your reading cloth to form a 'plus' sign/ symbol – or what could be described as a basic cross. This is not the same as the Runic Cross Layout, as that uses additional tiles.

When you're ready to start this reading, hold your bag of runes in your hand and gently shake them to mix them up. Think about what question you'd like answered, keeping in mind that this layout is particularly beneficial for dealing with queries related to situations or events.

When you're ready, start by pulling out the first rune one and placing it on the left hand side of the centre. Continue pulling out the runes, one by one, placing runes two and three side by side by the first rune to form a row (the same as how they appear in the Three Rune Layout).

The fourth rune is placed underneath the middle one (rune 2) and the fifth above the middle rune to form the plus sign or cross shape.

Once your chosen runes are laid out on your cloth, it's time to consider what messages they could be relaying. The position of the runes in this layout represent:

1 – The rune in position one relates to the current or present view of the situation.

2 – The rune in position two represents an obstacle or challenge that you may be facing and that could be deterring your progress.

THE FIVE RUNE LAYOUT
(CONTINUED)

3 – The third rune relates to the ultimate goal that you're aiming to achieve.

4 – The fourth rune represents the conscious or unconscious worries you may have about the situation.

5 – The fifth rune represents the potential final outcome that could occur.

You may find that the rune in position four is the trickiest one to analyze, especially if you don't consciously have any worries or concerns. The fact that there could be something looming in the background is likely to require more intuitive thinking to pull it to the surface. However, acknowledging its existence could help you break through any barriers you'd unconsciously put up and bring you one step closer to your ultimate goal.

Five Rune Layout.

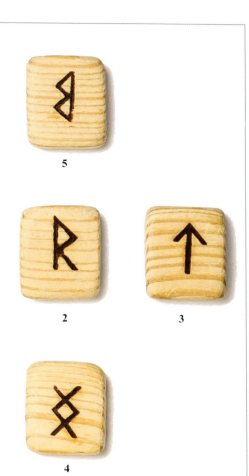

Example of how to do a Five Rune Layout.

THE SEVEN RUNE LAYOUT

How to do the Seven Rune Layout.

Seven is a significant number in Norse mythology, so it's only natural that a layout involving seven runes is a popular choice. This particular layout often goes by other names, including the Keystone Layout and the Runic V Layout, but it's essentially the same reading despite the different names. For this layout the runes are laid out in a V-shape, with the rune at position 4 – the base of the V – the keystone. As a keystone, it's regarded as being the most important rune in the layout. As well as being a keystone or building block for holding together both sides of the V layout, it's also seen as being the key to understanding the answers revealed in the reading.

If you're seeking more information from a reading, need help pondering a question or are seeking closure from a past experience or event, then the Seven Rune Layout is ideal. It may offer wisdom and insight into your present situation, how it's affected by the past and likely outcomes.

When you're ready to start this reading, think about what question you'd like to ask or the circumstances you'd like to focus on. Start by taking out the first rune and placing it in the top left of what will become the 'V' shape. Continue taking out another three runes, placing them in a downward diagonal shape. The fourth rune is the keystone and forms the base of the V. As you take out the fifth rune, it should be positioned rising diagonally upwards from the keystone, in line with the third rune. Runes six and seven will finish off the V-shape layout.

When all the runes are chosen and laid out on your reading cloth, explore the runes one by one to see what messages they could reveal.

Here's a guide to what each rune in the layout represents:

1 – The rune in the first position offers insight into the past and how it could still influence you.

2 – The rune in the second position offers insight into the present.

3 – The third rune can provide insight

THE SEVEN RUNE LAYOUT
(CONTINUED)

into your general prospects and hopes for the future.

4 – The keystone rune is the most crucial rune in this layout. The rune in this position represents the course of action you could take in order to achieve the best outcome.

5 – The fifth rune represents your feelings.

6 – The sixth rune highlights any potential problems that could delay or disrupt your plans.

7 – The seventh rune relates to the likely outcome.

If you want to connect more to the energies and messages of the keystone, you may like to keep the rune from this position in the reading close to you for a few hours. For example, you could pop it in your pocket or bag. This could help as you ponder the meaning and significance of the rune that appeared as your keystone.

Seven rune layout.

NINE RUNE CAST

The Nine Rune Cast differs from the other layout options as it doesn't involve a formal layout. It's often regarded as being one of the oldest forms of classical rune casts because a similar method was mentioned in the work of Roman writer Tacitus.

With this cast, it's even more important than usual to utilize your powers of intuition when reading the runes. Although there aren't formal positions in which to place each rune, there is some guidance available to help you read and analyze the runes and where they land.

This cast is useful for helping to answer questions relating to situations or circumstances that you're currently in, as well as indicating what factors from the past may have led you to where you are today.

To carry out a Nine Rune Cast, first find a quiet place to sit where you won't be disturbed and arrange your reading cloth on a table in front of you. Shuffle the runes in your bag, before putting one hand into the bag and randomly selecting nine runes. Hold the runes in your hand, while thinking about the question you'd like to ask.

When it feels like you're in a suitably receptive state of mind, cast or throw the runes onto your cloth. Ideally aim to be at least 15cm / 6in away from the table as you cast the runes; avoid using too much force as ideally you don't want the runes to fall off the table, although it's acceptable and not a cause for concern if the odd one does fall off. If some of the runes land upside down, don't worry, leave them where they land. Take a moment to look at which runic symbols you have in front of you and how and where the nine runes have fallen on your cloth. Some of the runes will have landed face up, but others might be face down. The runes in the centre of your cloth are regarded as the most important, as they are the closest to the issue or situation involved in your question. Allow plenty of time to study these runes, using your powers of intuition to analyze the messages.

Next, look at runes that are lying face up with their symbols showing on the edges of the cloth. These runes relate to

NINE RUNE CAST
(CONTINUED)

Example of a Nine Rune Cast with nine runes randomly positioned where they land.

the background influence that others may have on your question or on you and your situation. For example, some people may have strong opinions or feelings about something. If any runes have fallen off the cloth, you can discard these.

Now look at the runes that have landed face down. Turn them over one by one and read them in the order that you reveal their symbols. These runes relate to the future and potential outcomes.

Finally, look at all the runes on your cloth and see if you can spot any runes that seem to be positioned in pairs or groups. If there are any, these can be read as runic combinations, where the meanings are combined and amplified to add a deeper layer to your understanding. If you find this tricky, it's fine to leave this part of the analysis until your rune reading experience develops further.

Old divination by runestones.

THE RUNIC CROSS LAYOUT

Whereas most of the runic reading layouts use odd numbers, the Runic Cross Layout differs in that it uses an even number of runes – in this case, six. The runes are laid out to form the symbol of a runic cross, made up of a long vertical column and shorter horizontal arm.

This particular style of reading is useful if you're seeking a more in-depth response to a question. It explores potential factors of influence from the past and present, as well as identifying challenges, hopes and fears that could affect your path.

As with doing any form of runic layout, it's important to clear your mind of any preconceptions and clutter first, so that you're in the best frame of mind to perform a reading. You might want to meditate for a few moments as well and tune into your powers of personal intuition.

Hold your bag of runes in your hands as you think about the question for which you're seeking answers. When you're ready, randomly pick out the first rune and place it on the left, where it will form the left-hand horizontal arm of the cross. Next, pick the second rune and place it diagonally to the right, below what will become the centre of the layout (where rune five will sit).

Rune three should be placed to the right of central point. The fourth rune is placed below the rune in position two, to form the long vertical column of the cross. Rune five goes in the central position, at the heart of the cross and rune six sits above it. If you're concerned about getting the runes in the right positions, sketch out a plan on paper beforehand, so you can place the runes onto each numbered position.

When you've randomly chosen the runes from your bag and laid them out in order on your reading cloth to form the runic cross, it's time to delve deeper into the messages they could be offering you.

To help you analyze and understand the reading, this is what each rune in the layout represents:

1 – The rune in the first position represents the past and the influence it can have on the present and the question or issue you're dealing with.

2 – The rune in position two represents the present.

3 – The rune in position three represents your hopes and fears and how you imagine the future to be.

4 – The fourth rune focuses on the foundation of the matter, issue or question you've asked and includes any unconscious elements that could be involved.

5 – The rune in position five represents any obstacles, challenges or potential problems that could affect your aims or plans.

6 – The sixth and final rune represents the likely eventual outcome.

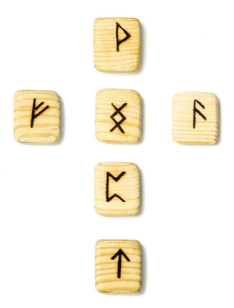

THE MAGIC SQUARE LAYOUT

The Magic Square Layout is an interesting runic reading layout involving nine runes. It's sometimes also referred to as the Nine Square Layout and is in effect an extended version of the Three Rune reading, but this time with more detailed information relating to events, people, desires and unconscious motivations and the impact these factors could have on the past, present and future.

The pattern of this layout forms a 3 x 3 grid and the runes are drawn and placed in certain positions on each row. The order of placement can seem confusing, so it may be helpful to sketch out a plan of where each rune needs to be placed before you embark on this reading. Once you've done it a few times, you're likely to remember more clearly where each rune should go. The runes should be read in the order in which they are placed onto the grid, from one to nine.

Follow your usual routine of preparing for a reading, by finding an appropriate place to sit quietly and focus your mind. Hold your bag of runes in your hands, while thinking of the question you'd like answered. Slowly select nine runes and place them on the magic square grid in the order shown.

The runes on the top row of the square – 4, 9 and 2 – reveal secrets relating to your potential future. The runes on the middle row of the square – 3, 5 and 7 – provide insight into the present. The runes on the bottom row of the magic square – 8, 1 and 6 – relate to issues in your past.

The messages in the runes are read as follows:

1 – The rune in position one relates to issues in your past and the influence it may still have on your present situation.

2 – The second rune relates to your future state of mind and the likely attitude you will have to the eventual outcome.

3 – The third rune focuses on hidden and unconscious factors in the present you might be unaware of, but could influence the events or situations in your life.

4 – The fourth rune focuses on how the hidden influences could affect the outcome of the question you've asked.

5 – Rune five reveals the present circumstances in your life.

6 – Rune six reflects your memories, opinions and attitudes to things that happened in the past.

7 – The rune in position seven focuses on your present beliefs, feelings and attitudes.

8 – The eighth rune relates to hidden secrets or unconscious influences that could have affected past events.

9 – The final rune relates to the best possible outcome to your question.

Whatever rune casting layout you're following, it's good to have a dedicated rune reading cloth on which to lay out your runes. A plain white cloth was traditionally used, but you can use any cloth you'd like; the key thing is to ensure it's a plain and uncluttered design so that you can focus your thoughts purely on the runic symbols and not be put off by anything else clouding your vision.

You can create an ambience for conducting your rune readings if you wish, including lighting candles or burning incense, but it's up to you and is by no means necessary.

It's interesting to note the significance of the numbers of runes used in layouts. Odd numbers featured widely in Norse mythology, in tales relating to Gods, people and events, and were also used extensively with rune casts. Some numbers, such as nine and three are regarded as being even more important symbolically than others.

The number nine, for example, is important for Norse cosmology, as nine worlds were believed to be supported by Yggdrasil, the World Tree. When the great god Odin sacrificed himself, he spent nine days and nights hanging on the gallows, before receiving runic secret knowledge. Likewise, references to the number three occur frequently in tales passed down by generations. There were three original beings, three Norns (goddesses of fate) and three sacred wells under Yggdrasil.

Runes as Talismans

Runic inscriptions were traditionally found carved into objects such as battle swords, silver chalices or items of jewellery in order that they could be carried or worn by their owner. These were then used as talismans to bring the wearer luck or protection.

It's not uncommon for runes to still be used in a similar way today, with symbols often added to pendants, rings, bracelets and other objects. As well as serving a decorative design purpose, for those akin to using runes, it can feel significant to have a favourite runic symbol adorning a special piece of jewellery.

If there's a particular runic symbol that you feel resonates more with you than others, then this can be a good choice for a talisman. For example, it may be that it's the meaning of the symbol that you feel strongly attached to. Or it may be that there's a particular symbol that evokes feelings of joy, strength, vitality, protection or love, for example. Due to the strong connection you have with the symbol, this is sometimes also called a personal power symbol. You can make your own talisman by painting, drawing or carving the runic symbol onto a pendant – such as small rounded piece of wood, flat pebble, piece of sea glass or flat piece of crystal. The finished item can be added to a necklace and worn around your neck, or added to a bracelet as a charm.

Image depicting the Sacrifice of Odin, as described in Norse mythology, by Frølich (1895).

Alternatively, you could have a special piece of jewellery made for you by a craftsperson; the symbols work well etched into pewter, solid silver or silver clay pieces, for example. Or, if that's not an option, look out for ready-made pieces of jewellery that include your favourite runestone on them. If you're not a fan of wearing jewellery, you can still create your own talismans to keep near you in other ways.

Runic symbols lend themselves perfectly to artworks. Look out for ready-made pictures, posters or postcards featuring runes that you could put up in your home and use as wall art. Have them on your desk, by your bed or in other prominent positions where you'll see them regularly.

If you like creating your own art, you could try your hand at producing your own pieces of runic art. For example, runestone symbols can be drawn, painted, sculpted or embroidered into handmade projects that you can display or use in your home. The abundance of print-on-demand services means that it's now easier than ever before to have designs printed onto all manner of objects, including mugs, wall art, t-shirts or sweatshirts. As long as the design can be uploaded onto your computer and saved as an image file (such as a JPEG or PNG), and the quality is good enough for print purposes, it can be printed onto a useable item.

However you choose to incorporate runes into your life and celebrate the symbols as talismans, be creative and find ways that are personal to you.

Pendant featuring a figure of the Norse god Odin and runic symbols.

Storing Runes

When runes aren't in use, they're best stored together in a dedicated storage vessel. Traditionally they are stored in a small fabric pouch, and this is still a popular option today, with many rune sets including a dedicated storage pouch. The pouch can be made of any fabric, but common choices include pure cotton, silk, velvet, hessian or linen, often with a simple drawstring tie. Pouches can be made of plain or decorated fabrics, such as with runic symbols. The pouch or bag simply needs to be big enough to hold a full set of runes so that they're kept safe when not in use. If you don't have a suitable pouch available, a useful alternative is a small wooden or metal box. The key issue is to ensure that they're kept together in the set, so you know exactly where they are when you want to use them.

Some people like to store crystals in with their runes when they're not being used. The theory is that certain crystals can have the ability to keep the energy of the runes cleansed, pure and protected. One of the best crystals for this is clear quartz. If you want to use it for this purpose, it's a good idea to cleanse and purify the crystal first.

A clear quartz crystal can be cleansed in various ways, but popular methods include holding it under cool running water, putting it on a windowsill under the light of the moon, burning a sage smudge stick or incense stick and letting the smoke waft over the crystal, or washing it in fresh seawater. Do be aware that some crystals, such as fluorite, calcite and selenite are water soluble, so shouldn't be placed in or underwater.

While it's always a good idea to store your runes in an easily accessible storage pouch or box, there may be times when you feel the need to be inspired by your runes on a regular basis and want to see them more often by displaying them.

Rune Altars

One of the ways in which you can celebrate your runes is to create a sacred space or rune altar. Sacred spaces have been an integral part of multiple spiritual, religious and cultural beliefs for centuries and offer a chance to display and celebrate items that have special meaning and importance.

You can create your own sacred space or rune altar anywhere in your home – it could be on a shelf, windowsill, mantelpiece or corner of a desk – it just needs to be clean, clutter-free and undisturbed. You could lay out some of your favourite runes or pick out a single rune that you feel most aligned with; if you have a spare set of runes, you may wish to use these instead of your regular set.

Make your rune altar unique and special by adding some of your favourite photos, artwork or quotations to your display. You could include crystals and objects you've found in nature, such as fir cones, shells, driftwood, pebbles or flowers. If you've created a talisman or artwork involving runes, this is a great place to have them on display. It doesn't have to stay the same all the time – you can change it with the seasons or when you feel the need to focus on different runes.

The overall idea is that your rune altar will become a special sacred place where you can feel motivated, inspired or uplifted when you look at it or interact with the items on it.

Making Your Own Runes

If you can't find a set of runes that you like, have had a basic set for a while and want to upgrade to something more personal, or simply fancy putting your creative or artistic skills to good use, then you could have a go at making your own set.

Runes can be made from a variety of materials, including small flat pebbles, shells, offcuts of wood, small pieces of glass, metal, leather or flat crystals. Natural materials are more in line with traditional runes, but it's fine to use whatever materials or recycled items you acquire. If you're keen on using wood, look out for small round or square pre-cut wooden tiles in a craft store, or for glass, pre-cut mosaic tiles work well.

To make a set of Elder Futhark runes, you'll need 24 pieces of material – plus one extra if you want to include a Wyrd (blank) rune. Ideally the runestones should be about the same size and you need to be able to comfortably fit them all in your hand.

Bear in mind that the runes will be more comfortable to use and handle if you choose materials that are smooth and tactile. If there are rough edges, such as on pieces of wood offcuts, take time to work on them and sand them down to make sure they're smooth before you start putting the runic symbols onto them.

Materials

The symbols for your runestones can be carved, painted, engraved, drawn or soldered onto your chosen materials.

If you're painting or drawing the symbols on, you may wish to consider adding a top layer of clear varnish once they're dry. The varnish will protect the design on your runestones and help improve their longevity. Likewise, if your runestones are made from wood, you can help protect the surface by adding a wood sealant product on top at the end (for example, linseed oil or beeswax).

Creating your own runestones gives you the opportunity to make a set that's unique and personal to you. You can choose to make the whole set uniform in colour, or use a rainbow of different colours for each symbol. Some people like to use three colours for the symbols, separating them into each of their aetts. It can be a therapeutic and artistic process to make your own runestones and one that may help you feel closer to the history, tradition and magic

Store your runes safely, for example, in a cloth pouch or wooden box.

of runes. Your familiarity with each symbol may become clearer as you carve, paint or draw each one onto your runestones and the end result is likely to be a set that you treasure.

Once they are completed, and you've found something suitable to store them in, it's also time to start aligning your energy to your new runestones. Make time to sit and handle your runes, get to know how the texture of them feels in your hands and how any particular runes make you feel. Practise some simple rune casts, such as the single rune cast, and boost your familiarity and confidence with using your new set.

MATERIALS

Depending on what you're using to make your runestones, some of the additional materials you may need include:

Fine paintbrushes
Marker or paint pens
Paint
Sandpaper
A carving tool, such as a knife or electric gadget
A pyrograph wood burning tool
Varnish
Wood sealant
Safety glasses – essential if you're cutting any materials

THE RUNIC ALPHABET

Opposite: Set of carved wooden runes from the Anglo-Saxon Futhorc..

The Elder Futhark
The Elder Futhark (pronounced 'footh-ark') is believed to be the oldest form of runic alphabet. It was widely used and developed in parts of Europe, including northern Germany and Scandinavia, by Germanic tribes during the 3rd to 5th centuries. It was used as both a form of symbolism and as an alphabet for writing.

The Futhark gets its name from the first six runes in the alphabet – Fehu (f), Uruz (u), Thurisaz (th), Ansuz (a), Raido (r) and Kaunaz (k) – which combined spell the word 'Futhark'.

There are 24 runes in the Elder Futhark, although over the years an additional blank rune – known as the Wyrd – has been added, which brings the total to 25. It is enitrely a matter of personal choice as to whether or not you decide to include the blank rune in your readings. The runes in the Elder Futhark are divided into three groups of eight, or aetts / aettir. These are called Frey's Aett, Hagal's Aett (also known as Heimdall's Aett) and Tyr's Aett.

The word 'aett' comes from the old Norse word for families. Used in this way, the aetts refer to the way the runes are grouped into families of related rune types. Each of the runes included in each of the aetts is there for a reason.

No one knows for certain exactly how or why each of the runes got their individual names, however, it is understood that runes in the Elder Futhark often tend to relate to popular elements of Norse mythology, including named gods or goddesses. For example, Frey's Aett is believed to derive its name from the Norse god Frey.The meanings of runes tend to be traditionally associated with issues that have typically affected people throughout history, such as health, food, wealth and fertility, as well as matters of the natural environment, including the effect of elements such as rain and air. Even though these meanings were conceived centuries ago, these issues remain valid for society today, although some meanings do require a degree of interpretation. For example, the rune Fehu can symbolize cattle, which were a key concern centuries ago but are generally less important to most people today. However, cattle are believed to represent prosperity and wealth, which are still relevant.

The period of use most commonly associated with the Elder Futhark is the Migration Period, from the 3rd to 5th centuries. This name reflects the large-scale movements of people across Europe during this period, in communities such as the Angles, Saxons, Jutes and Goths.

Although the Elder Futhark is best known for its use by people living in Scandinavia, it was also believed to be used in northern Germany and in countries such as Romania, Poland and Ukraine.

Some people like to light candles when reading the runes.

A wooden amulet featuring the kenaz, fehu and wunjo runes.

Frey's Aett Runes
Frey's Aett runes is the name given to the first group of eight runes, or aettir, that appear in the Elder Futhark.

The runes found in Frey's Aett are:

***Fehu* (f)**
***Uruz* (u)**
***Thurisaz* (th)**
***Ansuz* (a)**
***Raido* (r)**
***Kaunaz* (k)**
Gebo
Wunjo

When the first letters of the first six runes are put together, they form the word 'Futhark'.

Although there are 24 runes altogether in the Elder Futhark, breaking them down into three sets of aettir allowed the early users of runes to group them together into common themes. Each of the runes in the aett were chosen for a logical reason – it was by no means a random selection – and they're regarded as being in the same family of meaningful themes.

When viewed together as a whole, each of the runes in Frey's Aett builds on the meaning of the others, which together provide a wider perspective and better understanding. You could think of each rune being like an individual building block. They have their own specific use, meanings and purpose, but when they're put together, they create a bigger picture.

The three aett's in the Elder Futhark are all named after important gods and goddesses in Norse mythology. Frey's Aett gets its name from Frey (sometimes spelled Freyr), the god of peace, fertility and prosperity.

The runes in Frey's Aett represent creation, the foundation of life and making sense of your role in life. The runes focus on worldly issues such as prosperity, travel, generosity, courage, boundaries, insight and love.

FREY'S AETT RUNES

F

Fehu
Pronounced: Fay-who
Translation: Cattle, wealth
Key themes: Abundance, prosperity, wealth, new beginnings

Fehu is the first rune in Frey's Aett and its literal translation is 'cattle' (because the two points on the runic symbol are reminiscent of cattle horns). Fehu was associated with the great primeval cow Audhumla in Norse mythology, who brought the first Norse god into being. Cattle were regarded as an important measure of wealth for ancient tribes, therefore modern interpretations focus on the themes of wealth, prosperity and abundance. Depending on the context of the reading, this could mean monetary wealth and finances, but it could also relate to other means of prosperity and abundance in your life, such as good health, general well-being, being successful in your job, having a roof over your head or being in a loving partnership.

FREY'S AETT RUNES

SEEING FEHU appear in a reading could indicate abundance to come, especially if you have been through a difficult period, but it also serves as a reminder to be thankful for all that is thriving in your life. It can highlight the importance of managing your resources sensibly too, so it may serve as an indicator to look at practical ways to protect your prosperity so that you can use it wisely to enjoy life comfortably, without worries and anxiety.

Fehu also acts as a reminder to never take prosperity for granted and to value the importance of sharing wealth with family, friends and community. Greed is a negative behaviour, and Fehu is all about positivity.

As it's the first rune in the Elder Futhark and is linked to Audhumla, the appearance of Fehu can also signify new beginnings. It could be the case that something new is on the horizon for you, or that a new door of opportunity could be opened.

Old drawn image featuring Buri and Audhumla from the SAM 66 manuscript, held by the Árni Magnússon Institute for Icelandic Studies.

FREY'S AETT RUNES

Uruz
Pronounced: Oo-roose
Translation: Auroch (wild ox)
Key themes: Strength, energy, courage, vitality, health, motivation

The rune Uruz translates as 'aurochs', or European ox, which were wild and fierce animals (now extinct), known for their immense strength, power and energy.

It's therefore logical that the runic symbol named after such a beast represents strength, energy, vitality, courage, health and motivation. Although Uruz has traditionally been regarded as a masculine energy, the powerful themes within the rune are appropriate to anyone.

If you've suffered illness or any kind of loss of vitality, Uruz could signify healing and an improvement in strength – physically, emotionally or mentally. If health is not an issue,

FREY'S AETT RUNES

Uruz can represent the power of determination, and reflect the fact that you possess the strength within yourself to cope with whatever you're going through and that obstacles in life can be overcome with the right frame of mind.

If Uruz comes up in a reading, it can also be a motivating and encouraging rune. If there's something you've been thinking of doing, or if you are contemplating embarking on a new venture, Uruz could be a sign that you have the inner strength and courage to step into the unknown and give it a go.

Aurochs were wild and untamed, so Uruz can also serve as a reminder to rein in your energies because misdirected power can have negative effects. Too much power can be damaging, cause arrogant behaviour and lead you off your intended path. Instead, it's important to learn to respond appropriately to situations or circumstances you may find yourself in and to avoid letting power or strength go to your head. Remember the well-known saying, don't be a 'bull in a china shop'.

The head of an auroch carved on the pedestal of a statue of Stephen III in Chisinau, Moldova.

FREY'S AETT RUNES

THURISAZ

Thurisaz
Pronounced: Thoo-ree-sahz
Translation: Thorn, Thor and his hammer
Key themes: Boundaries, limitations, defence, protection, challenge, balance

The literal translation of Thurisaz is 'thorn', but it's also associated with the giant Norse thunder god, Thor, who famously carried a hammer, the symbol of his power (the 'thurs' part of the word 'Thursday' also derives from Thor).

The shape of this runic symbol looks like a thorn on a branch. Thorn bushes were traditionally used to divide land, therefore Thurisaz can be seen to represent boundaries and protection.

If Thurisaz appears in a reading, it could relate to both physical, mental, emotional or spiritual boundaries. For example, it might serve as a reminder to be careful about crossing the lines in a certain situation or a warning that you need to put your boundaries up to protect yourself from unwanted attention or opinions.

Thor's hammer is a symbol of destruction or defence, so Thurisaz can also be an indicator of a situation, person or view that could pose challenges in your life. The idea of destruction doesn't have to be a negative energy, however. It could be a cleansing and cathartic force to help you recover from an experience or event.

In Norse mythology, Thor took on the Giants. He didn't slay them all, but enough to create balance in the realm, so this symbol could serve as a reminder of the importance and need for balance.

If you're facing a challenge or need to make a decision, the energy of Thurisaz highlights the importance of considering your options carefully, thinking about your boundaries and ensuring that any decision retains the necessary balance.

Thor wielding his legendary hammer against the Giants.

FREY'S AETT RUNES

A

Ansuz
Pronounced: Ahn-sooze
Translation: A god
Key themes: Communication, wisdom, knowledge, signals, messages, writing, speaking, singing listening, expression, intuition

The fourth rune in Frey's Aett is Ansuz. The name translates as god and some people believe it could relate to the great Norse god Odin himself. Odin is regarded as the god of words, wisdom and communication, and these are the key themes at play in the runic symbol Ansuz.

On a practical level, Ansuz is a symbol of the importance of clear communication, whether it be writing, speaking, listening or even singing, along with the basic need to be able to express how you think and feel. Good communication is at the heart of life and forms an integral part of living, growing and working with others.

FREY'S AETT RUNES

If Ansuz appears in a reading, it may be related to issues surrounding work or the need to listen and communicate more with others. It could also be a signal to look out for messages of guidance in various forms, whether a letter, email, phone call or text. The energy of Ansuz is positive, but it is also a reminder of the importance of making sure that what other people are communicating is true and not taking everything at face value or without fully understanding what could be at stake.

Ansuz can also signify links with divine communication, the higher realms and the development of stronger spiritual connections. It may encourage you to work on your spiritual needs more or it could be an indicator to listen more to and take note of your intuition and divine wisdom.

The god Odin depicted with his ravens from the Poetic Edda – a collection of Old Norse poems from the Icelandic medieval manuscript Codex Regius.

FREY'S AETT RUNES

Raido
Pronounced: Rah-ee-do
Translation: Riding
Key themes: Travel, journey, changes,
movement, time, reunion, wheel of life

Raido is the fifth rune in the Frey's Aett family – it's sometimes spelled Raidho – and its literal translation means 'riding'. This is the rune of travel, which includes physical, emotional or spiritual journeys.

When Raido appears in a reading, it could signify that you're going to undergo a type of journey in your life. This could relate to a holiday or trip, an actual type of journey (such as getting the bus to work instead of driving), moving house or simply to the way you are journeying through life.

Raido represents a wheel, which could be seen as the wheel of life, or the wheels turning on a form of transport. Either way,

FREY'S AETT RUNES

the key energy of Raido involves movements and change. It reminds us that there are many different forms of journey, that journeys can vary and that everyone is at different stages.

Journeys don't always go as planned and life can take many twists and turns, so Raido is also a reminder to persevere with your journey whatever obstacles you may encounter. It can be a signal that you're on the right track, even if it doesn't always feel like it. Whatever your journey involves, it's important not to lose track of the bigger picture, or why you're undertaking a particular journey. What might be the right path for you may not apply to others, so don't be afraid of branching off in the direction that feels right for you.

Some interpretations of Raido suggest it could also mean a reunion. For example, it could be a sign that you'll have the chance to reconnect with old friends, family or colleagues.

Fortune's wheel depicted in a 15th-century fresco by Albertus Pictor in Härkeberga Church, Uppland, Sweden.

FREY'S AETT RUNES

K

Kaunaz
Pronounced: Kay-nahz
Translation: Torch
Key themes: Enlightenment, knowledge, light, insight, illumination, passion, manifestation

The sixth rune in Frey's Aett is Kaunaz – also spelled Kenaz – and its literal translation means 'torch'. For ancient civilizations, fire was an essential source of light and heat. Torches were commonly burned in homes to provide light to cook or perform other tasks, and were carried around when moving outside at night to spread light in the darkness. It's also linked to fire beacons, which were an important way of spreading messages and signals across long distances.

In runic symbolism, Kaunaz represents knowledge and enlightenment – both the receiving and passing on of them. It could be that you experience a sudden moment of enlightenment when you get an amazing idea, gain new insight into a situation or go through a period of illumination when everything makes sense. Someone may be sharing their knowledge with you and it could be a sign that you need to be open to receiving it and letting it into your mind. Enlightenment can take many forms, from physical elements to mental, emotional and spiritual ones.

Kaunaz can also represent a flame of passion – it could be the ignition of a new flame or the growth of an existing passion. This doesn't necessarily refer to romantic love; it could also indicate other types of passion, for example, creative passion, passion for an idea or feeling passionate about a new direction in life.

The symbol of Kaunaz is often likened to the 'greater than' symbol we use today, so it's sometimes associated with the idea of manifestation too. Overall, it's a positive, uplifting and encouraging symbol that reminds us of the need to be open to receiving enlightenment and passion in all its many and diverse forms.

Fragment of an old marble krater that shows Artemis carrying a torch representing the Goddess of Night and Darkness and a quiver as the Goddess of the Hunt.

FREY'S AETT RUNES

Gebo
Pronounced: Ghe-boo
Translation: Gift
Key themes: Generosity, gift, talents, transaction, affection, exchange, offering, contract

The seventh rune in Frey's Aett is Gebo, which literally means 'gift' and is known as the rune of giving and generosity. It represents the act of giving or receiving gifts in a transaction between people.

Gifts don't have to be tangible or in physical form; they can involve the giving of time, help, thoughts, love or talents. Spiritual gifts were also important to ancient peoples, who believed that the gods provided them with gifts, especially if they made an offering to them. For example, offerings were often made in the past to the Norse gods and goddesses such as Frey (or Freyr) and Freyja, the god and goddess of love and fertility.

FREY'S AETT RUNES

If Gebo appears in a reading, it could signify that some form of gift is coming your way – either physically, emotionally or spiritually. Or it could be a sign that you have a gift to share; it's a positive human trait to be generous with your talents, time and abilities, as well as share monetary wealth with other people or charitable organizations.

Not all gifts are always wanted or have to be accepted.Gebo could therefore serve as a reminder to think before you accept and follow due diligence in certain situations because not all gifts are made with a pure heart or mind. It may be beneficial to consider your own giving habits too and explore whether you're giving away too much, or even too little.

In written form, the runic symbol is an X. It's the same symbol that people use to sign documents when they're illiterate, as well as the symbol used to signify a kiss, so Gebo can also be associated with contracts and affection.

Freia the Germanic Goddess of love, youth and beauty, shown picking apples from a tree. Image by Arthur Rackham.

FREY'S AETT RUNES

W

Wunjo
Pronounced: Woon-yo
Translation: Joy
Key themes: Joy, bliss, romance, pleasure, fun, harmony, happiness, good fortune, security

Wunjo is the final rune in Frey's Aett and completes the journey through this set of runes on a happy, uplifting and high note for this is the rune of joy.

Wunjo can represent joy in all areas of your life, from personal relationships, family and your general life outlook to business and work dealings. It could signify that a new romance is on the cards, or that an existing relationship may deepen to new levels, but it also represents happiness, bliss and harmony in areas such as friendships, hobbies and feelings.

If you've been feeling down or dissatisfied with something recently, Wunjo could act as a reminder to try and find the things

FREY'S AETT RUNES

in your life that give you joy. You may need to make changes to your habits or attitudes in order to bring more joy back into your life, but it will be worth it if it puts a smile on your face.

In terms of friendships, Wunjo recognizes the importance of having fun, feeling secure and nurturing true friendships. It may act as a sign that it could be the time to find more of these significant friendships and connections.

If business or work partnerships are on your mind, then Wunjo could signify that new contracts or existing dealings may be fruitful and lead to good fortune for all concerned. Good fortune could be in monetary terms, but also in a mental, emotional or spiritual sense.

Wunjo builds on some of the elements witnessed in the other runes in Frey's Aett, especially Gebo (generosity), and serves as a reminder that good fortune and joy is best shared with others.

"The frolic of the Rhine-Maiden," 1910, by artist Arthur Rackham.

HAGAL'S AETT RUNES

Hagal's Aett Runes

Hagal's Aett runes – sometimes known as Heimdall's Aett – are the second set of eight runes found in the Elder Futhark.

The runes in Hagal's Aett are:

Hagalaz
Nauthiz
Isa
Jera
Eihwaz
Pertho
Algiz
Sowelo

Hagal's Aett gets its name from the Norse god Hagal. Little is known about Hagal, but some people believe he could in fact be Heimdall, the watchman of the gods – hence why Hagal's Aett is also often referred to as Heimdall's Aett. Regardless of what you choose to call this aett, the meanings and significance of the runes included within it remain the same.

The runes in Hagal's Aett were grouped together as they represent life's growth and how you adapt and mature in response to situations and circumstances that life throws at you. As you'll no doubt know, not everything in life goes smoothly and even the best-laid plans can be disrupted, often by circumstances beyond our control. Such instances are covered by the symbolic meanings of the runes in this aett with, for example, meanings such as obstacles, fate, disruption, progress, chance and celebration. Together the runes serve as a reminder that life always has ups and downs for everyone and, no matter how difficult it can be to navigate your way through, life changes and nothing lasts forever.

The eight runes together form a relevant and important family of meanings, but they have a wider significance too. As you begin to look at the rune meanings alongside those of Frey's Aett, you can start to see a broader overview of the stages of life building up. When you explore the Elder Futhark as a whole, you will discover that the three aetts cover the complete cycle of life as well as the typical stages and scenarios faced by humankind.

HAGAL'S AETT RUNES

Runes can be read anywhere, including outside whilst connecting with nature.

HAGAL'S AETT RUNES

Hagalaz
Pronounced: Hah-gah-laz
Translation: Hail
Key themes: Disruption, change, force of nature, chaos, interruption, obstacles

Hagalaz is the ninth rune in the Elder Futhark and the first in the series of Hagal's Aett runes. Its literal translation means 'hail' or 'hailstone' and it's a rune associated with disruption.

Sudden changes in weather have always been a factor that can disrupt and change plans. For ancient Germanic tribes, who relied more on the land and growing their own crops, an unexpected hail storm could damage their harvest and may have been a sign that a period of worsening weather was on its way.

Hagalaz represents a force of nature – the sudden change and disruption that occurs when you least expect it – that's completely out of your hands. Life often plays a card that you least expect and that hadn't been foreseen. For example, poor weather or illness can throw your organized plans right off course.

If the question you've asked the runes involves starting something new or making a change in your life, it may suggest that it's worth waiting a bit until things settle down. The disruption won't necessarily be major, it might just be a temporary hiccup that can be resolved quickly.

Although the nature of Hagalaz appears negative, it also serves as a reminder to remain positive and optimistic when faced with any difficult circumstances. In the same way that hail doesn't last forever – eventually the sun shines again and melts the hail – other forms of disruption in life don't last forever either and you'll be blessed with better days too. So, if you do experience change and disruption, keep smiling and weather the storm with patience and perseverance, maintaining optimism that brighter days lie ahead.

A peaceful forest after a hailstorm.

HAGAL'S AETT RUNES

Nauthiz
Pronounced: Now-theez
Translation: Need, necessity
Key themes: Need, necessity, difficulty, survival, delay, lack, hardship

Nauthiz is the tenth rune in the Elder Futhark and represents the concept of needs and necessity.

Needs can take many forms, including physical, emotional and spiritual. If Nauthiz appears in a reading, it can encourage you to focus on the things you need in your life in order to make an assessment of what might currently be lacking. Nauthiz offers a reminder to focus on those things you really need, rather than on things you want or would like, as there's a distinct difference.

Germanic tribes often lit what they called a need-fire in times of worry, hardship or distress, such as during plagues or when crops failed, to try and ward off negativity and evil spirits. It can therefore also represent hardship in a form that might be limiting how you progress with plans, tasks or aims. You may feel restricted due to a lack of resources, time or money and feel held back from where you'd like to be or what you'd ideally like to be doing. It might serve as a signal that you need to re-evaluate your plans and circumstances or direct your energy more practically where it's needed.

Nauthiz can represent tricky times that cause difficulties and delays, but it also serves as a useful pointer that you can get through problems. Humans are adept at surviving and can help each other through challenging times. With the right focus, support and help you can learn to deal with failures and disappointments. As the saying goes, 'when one door closes, another one opens'.

Fortune's wheel depicted in a 15th-century fresco by Albertus Pictor in Härkeberga Church, Uppland, Sweden.

HAGAL'S AETT RUNES

Isa
Pronounced: Eee-sa
Translation: Ice
Key themes: Obstacles, coldness, delay, blockages,
pause, stillness, danger

Isa, the eleventh rune in the Elder Futhark, is once more traditionally weather-themed; its literal translation means 'ice'. In fact the shape of the rune resembles an icicle, although there is, of course, more to its symbolism than a weather prediction.

For Nordic tribes, ice could pose serious dangers. On the ground it could be treacherous to walk on, however, when water freezes over it can also stop the natural flow of water in rivers and springs limiting the source of fresh clean water. When glaciers form, they can cause blockages preventing the free movement of people. Thick ice can be powerful and cause disruption in many different ways.

HAGAL'S AETT RUNES

The runic symbol represents the notion of blockages and obstacles occurring that cause delays. If Isa appears in a reading, it may represent a period of stillness when things pause, even though this can be incredibly frustrating. It may be a work project that's been affected, a friendship or a house move. The energy of Isa reminds us of the importance of accepting potential obstacles, however chilly and uncomfortable they are, and learning to be patient while they resolve (or the ice melts).

Isa can also symbolizes emotional coldness. For example, there may be an active icy chill in romantic relationships, friendships or acquaintances with business colleagues. Or it might be that your approach is viewed by others as icy, even if it's unintentional. This could suggest that it's appropriate to look at your actions and how you express yourself to others.

A stunning view of icy fjords in Norway.

HAGAL'S AETT RUNES

Jera
Pronounced: Yair-are
Translation: Harvest, year
Key themes: Year, celebration, joy, goodwill, optimism, turning point, cycle, growth, fertility

Jera, the twelfth rune in the Elder Futhark, means 'harvest' or 'year'. The harvest was traditionally a crucial time in the annual cycle of life and work, with communities coming together to celebrate the harvesting of fields and gathering of crops – the fruits of their labour.

Jera is regarded as a symbol of celebration and positive milestones. It could relate to the successful end of a project or the excitement of a new one, for example, moving house, getting a new job, getting a place at college or having a baby. It highlights the positive feelings of achievement involved in reaping the benefits of rewards after hard work and the importance of taking

HAGAL'S AETT RUNES

stock and celebrating significant landmarks. It's also reminiscent of the relief felt for persevering through difficulties and coming out the other side in brighter times.

It doesn't go unnoticed that Jera is the fourth rune in Hagal's Aett and follows the tricky themes in the runes Hagalaz, Nauthiz and Isa, which can all signify issues relating to obstacles and disruption. If Jera appears alongside any of these runes, it's a positive sign that change for the better is on its way and that you'll soon experience a turning point in any hardship or adversity.

As it's associated with cycles of growth, Jera may also be seen as representing fertility, whether in terms of harvests, becoming pregnant or any other activities involved with creativity and personal growth. For example, it may be a fertile time for new plans or ventures to take shape.

A wall painting in Elmelunde, Denmark featuring characters from ancient legends engaged in harvesting.

HAGAL'S AETT RUNES

EIHWAZ

Eihwaz
Pronounced: Eye-wahz
Translation: Yew (tree)
Key themes: Tree of Life, protection, wisdom, progress, purpose, life cycle, change, death, rebirth

Eihwaz is the thirteenth rune in the Elder Futhark and it means 'yew tree' (it's sometimes also known as Eoh). The shape of the symbol represents hunting with a bow and arrow and bows were traditionally made from wood sourced from yew trees.

Eihwaz is associated with the Tree of Life (called Yggdrasil in Norse mythology) and the cycle of life, and it's regarded as a rune of progress. Yew trees are traditionally found in graveyards and are often linked to death, not least because they're toxic and have been used as an ingredient in poisons. Paradoxically, they can also represent life, thanks to their evergreen nature and longevity.

HAGAL'S AETT RUNES

This 'yin-yang' (two opposing and complementing principles) nature of yew trees reflects why the runic symbol of Eihwaz can represent endings and beginnings, such as life, death and rebirth. If it appears in a reading it doesn't mean an actual death will occur, but merely signifies some form of ending is likely. Rather than being negative, it's a positive and optimistic runestone, as the cycle of life continues to progress. When something ends – such as a period of your life, a job, a relationship or even a favourite pair of shoes – it provides the chance and space for new possibilities to occur. It might be tricky to see it at the time, but the ending of something could be paving the way to a new and improved life.

As bows and arrows are used to defend yourself, Eihwaz can also represent protection. It may signify protecting yourself from physical, emotional, mental or spiritual attack, or of the need to protect others.

Celtic and Norse inspired image of the Tree of Life.

HAGAL'S AETT RUNES

PERTHO

Pertho
Pronounced: Per-thow
Translation: Pawn, dice cup
Key themes: Chance, fate, destiny, luck, game of life, mystery

Pertho is the fourteenth rune in the Elder Futhark and the sixth in Hagal's Aett. It has acquired a reputation for being one of most mysterious runes, as its exact translation and meaning has been the subject of great debate over the years.

In Norse, the word 'Pertho' translates as 'pawn', but it's also thought to mean 'lot cup' (as in a dice cup for gaming). The shape of the rune resembles a kind of vessel or cup. The ancient Germanic people often used a cup to draw lots, such as for parcels of land, and the traditional rune casting method involves randomly throwing runes down, like you would dice from a cup. As such, Pertho is regarded as the rune of chance.

HAGAL'S AETT RUNES

Life can often seem like a game of chance, so if Pertho appears in a reading, it could be an indication that a chance in your life could pay off. Fate may provide you with a stroke of luck that could change your destiny. The gaming aspect also serves as a reminder to keep your cards close to your chest until you're completely sure of a situation, decision or person.

If you've been deliberating a choice or decision and are uncertain what to do, the appearance of Pertho could be a sign that you need to delve deeper and unleash your intuitive powers to work through it and uncover the mysteries. Going within yourself and clearing your mind of clutter can help you attune to the answers and gain a clearer picture. The game of life can seem like a mystery, but taking a chance and making moves may open up new opportunities.

Old table game originating from the Viking era, featuring counters made from hand carved antler.

HAGAL'S AETT RUNES

Algiz
Pronounced: Al-geez
Translation: Elk
Key themes: Protection, defence, self-interest, healing, willpower

Algiz is the fifteenth rune in the Elder Futhark and its literal translation is 'elk'. The shape of the Algiz rune symbol itself is believed to represent both the antlers of an elk and elk sedge – a very thorny, sharp-leaved swampy plant that elks enjoy eating.

If Algiz appears in a reading, it can be a sign of protection – that you don't need to fret or fear about the question you've asked. It doesn't mean that there's never any danger in any form, but if you keep your head clear and make sensible decisions, you could be protected from a negative outcome. It could also be a sign that you need to seek extra protection where possible; for example, by

HAGAL'S AETT RUNES

using your intuition or connecting to higher spirits, as the ancient Norse were fond of doing. Some say the symbol of Algiz is like putting your hands up and reaching out to connect with the divine.

It can also signify that you need to spend some time on yourself – that it will be in your self-interest to do so. For example, if you're always looking after other people and lead a busy stressful life, it may be that you need to spend some time on your own care and needs. It's not selfish, it's looking after you because your health and well-being matter too. This will give you more strength in the long run.

Algiz can also be connected with willpower. If you're about to start a difficult task, have a health concern or any other issues that are hard to deal with, the appearance of Algiz brings reassurance that you have the willpower to tackle whatever it is with grace and dignity.

Silhouette of an elk in a field.

HAGAL'S AETT RUNES

Sowelo
Pronounced: So-we-loh
Translation: Sun
Key themes: Success, power, victory, light, energy, enlightenment, vitality, joy, happiness, abundance, inspiration, triumph

Sowelo is the last rune in Hagal's Aett and represents the sun – a powerful symbol to the ancient Norse people. For the Norse, it was the sun goddess, Sunna, who brought her rays of warmth to help thaw the ice and impenetrable ground, enabling crops to grow and providing much needed light to help the community thrive.

This is a positive and encouraging rune, representing power, success and vitality. If Sowelo appears in a reading, it provides hope, joy and reassurance that even after the darkest times, light will once again shine through and brighter days will come.

HAGAL'S AETT RUNES

If you're pondering a tricky question, Sowelo could help shine a light on the situation and clear your mind of confusion. It can also be a sign of abundance, hinting that you're surrounded by joy, positive energy, happiness and success, even if you can't see it at present or are unaware of it. By clearing your body and mind of negative energies, you could help fill your body and soul with the positive joy and abundance you deserve.

The symbol of Sowelo looks like a flash of lightning, which can be seen as symbolizing illumination and enlightenment. Enlightenment is regarded as a power that comes from within, providing inspiration and illumination to thoughts, feelings and situations.

The power of the sun can be destructive – its rays burn – so Sowelo also represents triumph and victory. It can be a reminder too of the need to balance your energy. If you're putting too much energy into one area, you could become unbalanced. Remember to ground yourself and not take on too many commitments.

Carved stone image of the God Sunna, by John Michael Rysbrack (1694–1770).

Tyr's Aett Runes

The third and final aett in the Elder Futhark is Tyr's Aett. The eight runes found in this aett are:

Tiwaz
Berkana
Eoh
Mannaz
Laguz
Inguz
Othila
Dagaz

Tyr's Aett gets its name from the Norse god Tyr, who was revered as the god of war, law and justice.

The runes in Tyr's Aett were chosen to be grouped together because they represent both the development of spirituality and the legacy and importance of family and community ties. On the surface it may seem like an odd combination, however, alongside each other they can be seen as representative of both visible and invisible realms – the way they intertwine and the impact that both of these play on your life.

These issues are reflected by the symbolic meanings of the runes in Tyr's Aett. For example, the runes have keywords such as birth, commitment, potential, authority, ideas and loyalty. Together the runes serve as a reminder of some of the important elements of life.

Tyr's Aett can be viewed as an important family of related runes, but when it's put together with the other two aetts (Frey's and Hagal's), it forms an integral part of the Elder Futhark. Combined they represent some of the key issues people face in life and offer insight into how particular situations and circumstances could be dealt with. Of course, it's always important to keep in mind that you have your own free will, so the answers the runes reveal are never a definitive conclusion – you have the ability to make your own choices and decisions. Nothing is set in stone.

TYR'S AETT RUNES

A 16th-century Scandinavian engraving of a man holding 'training sticks'
– used for teaching people how to read and write runes.

TYR'S AETT RUNES

Tiwaz
Pronounced: Tee-wahz
Translation: Tyr (the god)
Key themes: Courage, strength, commitment, victory, justice, duty, responsibility, perseverance, discipline, warrior

Tiwaz is the first rune in Tyr's Aett and rather appropriately translates to mean the god Tyr, who was the Norse god of war and justice. He was famed in mythology for sacrificing his right hand in order to save Odin.

Tiwaz represents courage, strength and discipline; that you have the responsibility and duty to do your best in order to seek justice and achieve victory. If Tiwaz appears in a reading it could be a sign that you should honour your commitments, whether to family, work, relationships or friendships, and ensure any bonds aren't broken. If you're honest and just in all your actions, the right outcome will occur. If the question asked relates to issues

TYR'S AETT RUNES

about love, romance or marriage, this is a positive and encouraging rune to appear and signifies the importance of strong bonds between people in relationships.

The symbol on the Tiwaz runestone represents a spear, or an arrow pointing upward, and is the sign of a spiritual warrior. It's also regarded as being like a masculine male figure. If you're male and have asked the question, it could represent you; if you're female, it may relate to a close male figure in your life.

The overall energy of Tiwaz serves as a reminder that sometimes you need to put bigger causes and issues before your personal interests, in order to gain a greater benefit for the wider community.

The Poetic Edda is a collection of Old Norse poems primarily preserved in the Icelandic mediaeval manuscript, Codex Regius.

TYR'S AETT RUNES

Berkana
Pronounced: Ber-kahn-ah
Translation: Birch
Key themes: New beginnings, birth, fertility, rebirth, healing, nurturing

Berkana is the second rune in Tyr's Aett and the eighteenth runestone in the Elder Futhark. The translation of its name means 'birch', after the birch tree and the birch goddess.

Traditionally, a branch of the birch tree was used in springtime fertility festivals, so it makes sense that the runic symbol is associated with birth and new beginnings. The stone has a feminine energy and is said to represent the Great Mother, or the goddess Nerthus as the early Germanic people called her.

If Berkana appears in a reading, it can represent birth and new beginnings – not just physical birth, but any new starts that you're making. For example, a new job, a new relationship, new project or

TYR'S AETT RUNES

a new house, to name a few. Berkana represents rebirth and healing too; in the same way that a birch tree can rejuvenate itself after being cut and sprout new seedlings, so too can human beings experience healing and regeneration and grow further.

There are associations with fertility and physical birth and it could be a positive rune to see coming up in a reading relating to female reproductive health in particular. The caring aspect of motherhood and nurturing can also be reflected and could be an indication of the need to nurture others, as well as look after your own self-care needs.

If the person asking the question is female, then some people consider that Berkana could represent them. If it's a male asking the question, it's likely to represent a close female friend or relation.

Image of a birch tree, which the runic symbol Berkana is named after.

TYR'S AETT RUNES

Eoh
Pronounced: Ee-oh
Translation: Horse
Key themes: Trust, loyalty, commitment, partnership, cooperation, faithfulness, travel, change, progress

The third of the runes in Tyr's Aett, and the nineteenth in the Elder Futhark, is Eoh (sometimes also known as Ehwaz).

The Eoh rune represents a horse, a crucial animal in the lives of ancient Germanic people, who relied on horses for travel and daily tasks. Its symbol might look like an M at first glance, but is actually said to represent two horses standing and facing each other.

Just like the link between a horse and its rider, Eoh symbolizes the trust, loyalty, bond and cooperation involved in creating a strong and mutually beneficial partnership. For any form of partnership to be successful, both parties have to be committed, faithful and respectful of each other. When the two parties are in step with each other, great things can be achieved. However, if the partnership is unbalanced or one party dominates the other, the equilibrium is lost and the union is unlikely to be successful.

In the same way that horses gallop and move, Eoh can represent travel, change and new directions. It can signify a journey – either intentional or unexpected – and could perhaps involve unknown or unfamiliar terrain. It doesn't have to be a physical journey – it could be an emotional or spiritual form of journey or a journey you're making through different stages of your life. Whatever form of journey it may be, Eoh is an encouraging sign that tells you although change will happen and may be unsettling, progress will be made and you're on the right track.

Brunnhilde silently leads her horse down the path to the cave. Image from *The Rhinegold & the Valkyrie,* **illustrated by Arthur Rackham (1910).**

TYR'S AETT RUNES

Mannaz
Pronounced: Mah-nahz
Translation: Mankind
Key themes: Humankind, humanity, self, friendships,
human potential, morals, values, self-care, interdependence,
relationships

Mannaz means 'man' or humankind. The shape of the symbol reflects its meaning, as it looks rather like two people standing face to face. This rune is a reminder of the unique qualities that humans possess and the way in which individuals can become part of a community. Even though there are humans spread across the world, living in different countries and with different cultures and beliefs, everyone is essentially the same – part of humankind.

This focus on the self and on the importance of looking after your own needs for the greater good of your community is reflected in the meanings of the runic symbol. If Mannaz appears in a reading, it could be a reminder of the importance of self-care and self-awareness. It may be beneficial to stop and explore your physical, mental, emotional and spiritual needs and question whether you're meeting them as well as you could.

This rune can also highlight support from others and how sometimes you may need to accept assistance, even if you think you don't need it. If you fail to look after yourself, it can affect those around you. Although you're an individual, you have an interdependence with other people and mutual support is vital.

Mannaz can also relate to other forms of relationships and friendships, and may signify a need to take stock and assess whether the values and morals of others match yours.

Image depicting two people reaching out and holding hands, representing humanity.

TYR'S AETT RUNES

Laguz
Pronounced: Lah-gooze
Translation: Water
Key themes: Flow, abundance, intuition, the unconscious, growth, psychic abilities, love

Laguz is the twenty-first rune in the Elder Futhark and the fifth in Tyr's Aett. The name Laguz means water and is linked to Nerthus, the Norse goddess of water.

Water is one of nature's elements and it played a central role for the seafaring Norse people. Water is found all around us – in the ground and earth and up above in the skies. Laguz represents the ebb and flow of water in its many different forms. If it appears in a reading, it may act as a reminder of the importance to stop resisting the unknown and trying to control things around you – to instead let go and go with the flow. When there are no obstacles in the way, love and abundance will have a better chance of flowing into your life.

TYR'S AETT RUNES

Water is connected with human emotions too – crying is an emotion, for example, and tears can be cleansing – and Laguz reminds us that emotions can be conscious, unconscious or subconscious. Like water, we can't always control emotions and they need to be acknowledged and dealt with; hiding emotions away and ignoring them causes stagnation, whereas accepting them helps personal growth in many ways.

Laguz is also associated with intuition and psychic abilities. It encourages time spent 'going within' – learning to deepen your intuition and connect with your inner self. Learn to follow your personal intuition even in the face of logic and practicality, which may suggest otherwise, and be more receptive to messages from your higher realms.

The runic symbol Laguz means water and represents the ebb and flow of water.

TYR'S AETT RUNES

INGUZ

Inguz
Pronounced: Ing-uzz
Translation: The god Ing
Key themes: New beginnings, fertility, turning points, problem-solving, completion, home, family

Inguz is the sixth rune in Tyr's Aett and the twenty-second in the Elder Futhark. It derives its name from the male fertility god Ing (sometimes called Ingwaz). This rune is also linked to Frey (or Freyr), the twin brother of Freya, who was also known for masculine energy and fertility.

Inguz is often described as being the twin of the Berkana rune, since they are both connected with new beginnings and fertility. Whereas Berkana has female energy, however, Inguz is abundant with male energy. It can be a positive sign for male fertility.

If Inguz appears in a rune cast or rune layout, it could represent

TYR'S AETT RUNES

the completion of one thing and the start of something new. For example, it could relate to the completion of a project and the start of a new job, or be linked to new travel plans, friendships or relationships. If you've experienced a difficult problem, Inguz can be a sign that a solution is on the horizon. Rather than worrying about the problem, Inguz acts as a reminder that if you distance yourself from your anxieties, the solution could become clearer.

Inguz can also represent home and family and the comfort, protection and safety that a home provides. If you've had any worries about your home, living situation, safety or family, Inguz is a positive sign that all will be well in the long run.

**Old carved stone featuring images of Odin, Thor and Freyr.
From the Swedish History Museum in Stockholm.**

TYR'S AETT RUNES

Othila
Pronounced: Oh-thi-la
Translation: Heritage
Key themes: Heritage, inheritance, legacy, responsibility, identity, family ties, authority, tradition

The order of the last two runes in the Elder Futhark has been the subject of much debate. Some say that the twenty-third rune in the Elder Futhark and the seventh in Tyr's Aett is Othila (sometimes called Othala), whereas others believe it's Dagaz. Whatever your belief, ultimately their meanings are the same whichever way round they're listed.

For the ancient Norse, the concepts of family, heritage, kinship and legacy were vital. Othila represents these notions – the legacies that have been passed down through generations of families and communities, including family secrets, identity

TYR'S AETT RUNES

and ancestral wealth. It could signify the traits you share with your family or highlight difficulties in instances where older generations don't understand your lifestyle choices.

Othila doesn't just relate to families, though; it can represent the strong ties and connections with your wider tribe too, including work colleagues, team mates, religious groups or social connections. If Othila appears in a reading, it could signify the need to reach out to your extended tribe and rely more on them. It could also relate to the help you could provide them. For example, there may be situations where you could benefit from the advice of someone older, wiser or with similar experiences.

Learning to accept your own identity, take responsibility for yourself and find the right balance in terms of accepting old traditions and creating your own new ones are all as important now as they were to your ancestors.

"Hundling discovers the likeness between Siegmund and Sieglinde," from *The Rhinegold & the Valkyrie* illustrated by Arthur Rackham, published in 1910.

TYR'S AETT RUNES

Dagaz
Pronounced: Dahg-az
Translation: Daylight, dawn
Key themes: Illumination, enlightenment, hope, prosperity, strength, growth, well-being, happiness, transformation, insight

The last rune in the Elder Futhark, and the final in Tyr's Aett, is Dagaz, a rune of light and illumination. Its meaning translates to daylight or dawn. The symmetrical butterfly shape of the symbol represents the balance between opposites, like light and dark, and how equilibrium is achieved when things are equally balanced.

For the ancient Norse, daylight was revered and they kept records of when more daylight was due by following the patterns of the moon. Dagaz is associated with the winter solstice, which marks the shortest day of the year before a time when the darkness will gradually lessen.

TYR'S AETT RUNES

Placed as the final Elder Futhark rune, Dagaz can be regarded as being similar to the light coming out of darkness, the unleashing of burdens and the emergence into clarity and happiness. It represents transformation, hope, prosperity and well-being and is an appropriate stone for the culmination of a runic journey through the Elder Futhark.

If you've experienced difficult times physically, emotionally, mentally or spiritually, the appearance of Dagaz in a reading is a positive encouragement that you will come through stronger, happier and more hopeful. Your journey might not end immediately, but the right machinery is in place to ensure a positive outcome eventually. The link to light represents the illumination and enlightenment that can result from a journey, but it could also be related to artistic or creative enlightenment.

Daylight is also regarded as being a protective force, therefore Dagaz could also represent being guided and protected from danger.

Ale's Stones or Ales Stenar, megalithic monument near Ystad in southern Sweden.

The Anglo-Saxon Futhorc

As communities and individuals continued to migrate and invade other countries, such as the British Isles, by the 9th century the Elder Futhark had outgrown its original purpose. The runic alphabet now needed to serve and represent the needs of the different vocabulary sounds found in Old English, the language the Anglo-Saxons brought to Britain.

The process of change was very slow, but the original 24 runes are first thought to have developed into 26 runes, then 28. More runes were added at a later stage, bringing it up to a total of 33.

Like the Elder Futhark, the Futhorc gets its name from the first six runes in the alphabet – F, U, TH, O, R and C.

Some of the extra runes are believed to have been added to account for certain sounds that existed in Anglo-Saxon English, but had no place in Germanic languages, such as the sound, 'ng'. There are also extra runes to account for the way different dialects and abbreviations use different sounds.

As you can see, like the Elder Futhark, the meanings of the runes were generally simple and often featured nature, animals, weather or objects. All of them held great meaning to the society in which they were used and made it easy to simplify messages or inscriptions when written.

Copy of the Anglo-Saxon rune poem in George Hickes'
Linguarum veterum septentrionalium thesaurus grammatico-criticus et archeologicus.

The way the runic symbols in the Anglo-Saxon Futhorc are written differs from the Elder Futhark. Whereas the Elder Futhark focused on straight lines, the Futhorc features more curved lines. The lines themselves are unlikely to have strong significance, but instead are representative of the changing style of writing.

Similarly, when used for written purposes, the Elder Futhark was primarily written from left to right, whereas the Anglo-Saxon Futhorc was either written from left to right or right to left – a factor that can be highly confusing when it comes to translating inscriptions.

Knowledge about the runes has stemmed in part from the so-called Anglo-Saxon Rune Poem, which is believed to date from the 9th century. The original was sadly lost in a fire at Ashburnham House in Westminster, London, in 1731, but it described the meanings and importance of each of the runic symbols in poetic format.

The Anglo-Saxon Futhorc is believed to have been actively used in the British Isles until about the 10th century when its use declined.

FUTHORC RUNES AND THEIR MEANINGS

The 33 Futhorc runes and their meanings, where known, are:

1) *Feoh* – wealth
2) *Ur* – aurochs (wild ox)
3) *Þorn* – thorn
4) *Ōs* – god
5) *Rād* – ride
6) *Cēn* – torch
7) *Gyfu* – gift
8) *Wynn* – joy
9) *Hægll* – hail
10) *Nyd / Nēod* – need/plight
11) *Is* – ice
12) *Ger / Gēar* – year
13) *Eoh* – yew
14) *Peorð* – pear wood
15) *Eolhx* – elk
16) *Sigel* – sun
17) *Tiw* – god / planet Mars
18) *Beorc* – birch
19) *Eh* – horse
20) *Mann* – man
21) *Lagu* – lake
22) *Ing* – a hero
23) *Ēðel* – estate
24) *Dæg* – day
25) *Āc* – oak
26) *Æsc* – ash tree
27) *Yr* – bow
28) *Ior* – eel
29) *Ēar* – grave
30) *Ȳr* – bow
31) *Calc* – chalice
32) *Stan* – stone
33) *Gar* – spear

The Younger Futhark

The 9th century marked the beginning of what became known as the Viking Age. By this time the runic alphabet had again seen changes made to it as language and dialects altered, but this time, rather than adding in more runes, the number was reduced to only 16 runes. The resulting runic alphabet was called the Younger or Scandinavian Futhark and it was widely used throughout the Viking Age.

Ironically, the spoken language of the Germanic tribes had changed too, but whereas the number of vowels grew in their spoken language, the number of runes went down. This did at least help simplify the runic alphabet of the Younger Futhark as it would have been far too complicated if numerous additional runes were added.

According to researchers from the National Museum in Copenhagen, the 16 runes in the Younger Futhark and their meanings are:

1) Fé – cattle, wealth
2) Úrr – aurochs (wild ox)
3) Þurs – giant, troll
4) Áss – as, god
5) Reið – to ride, chariot
6) Kaun – boil, sore
7) Hagall – hail
8) Nauð – need, compulsion
9) Ís – ice
10) Ár – year
11) Sól – sun
12) Týr – the god Taurus
13) Bjarkan – birch
14) Maðr – man
15) Lǫgr – water
16) Ýr – yew

The three aetts were still used, but there were fewer runes in some of them. Frey's Aett still contained eight runes, but Hagal's Aett and Tyr's Aett both had four each.

As you can see, there are some similarities with the Elder Futhark, highlighting the way in which the runes have been derived. The meanings are also still associated with basic human needs, gods, animals and natural elements.

Some variations have been found between the runic symbols of the Younger Futhark, however, particularly between different countries in Scandinavia. In Denmark, the symbols were often produced in a standard or so-called 'long-branch' style, whereas in Sweden and Norway they were frequently found written in a simplified or 'short-twig' style. Similarly, the interpretation of their meanings can differ slightly too.

Experts disagree as to why these variations developed, with some suggesting that the long-branch style was used for writing inscriptions on stone runestones, whereas the short-twig style was used for inscribing short messages on wood or writing personal runic inscriptions.

Dalecarlian runic inscription from 1635 in Orsblecksloftet, Zorns gammelgard, Mora, Dalarna, Sweden.

During the Viking Age, more people began using the Younger Futhark, possibly due to an improvement in general literacy and thus greater awareness of the runic alphabet. As a result, thousands of ancient runestone inscriptions from this period have been found dotted across Scandinavia.

Use of the Younger Futhark runes declined when Catholicism was introduced into Scandinavia and by the 12th century, the majority of writing took the form of the Latin alphabet.

The use of runes didn't disappear completely however. Some communities still used runic inscriptions for magical or cultural purposes. In the central Swedish province of Dalarna, a Latin-style form of runes was developed using a mix of runic and Latin alphabets. It was thought to have originated in the early 16th century and was used up until the early 20th century. These runes are referred to as Dalrunes or Dalecarlian runes and more than 200 inscriptions, mostly on wood, have been discovered.

124

Map of the Northern Regions– in *Theatrum Orbis Tearrarum* by Ortelius, 1570.

ANCIENT RUNSTONES

Opposite: Part of the Rök runestone (Rökstenen) in Sweden, which features one of the longest known runic inscriptions.

Runestones and Runic Inscriptions

Ancient runestones and their runic inscriptions help provide a crucial glimpse into life in ancient times and enhance our understanding of the past. The majority of runestones have been discovered in Scandinavia, namely in parts of Sweden, Denmark and Norway, although as the Norse people migrated and travelled, runestones appeared in other parts of the world too, including the British Isles, Eastern Europe and Russia.

In Scandinavia, by far the most known stones and fragments with inscriptions (numbering thousands) have been discovered in Sweden. This may be down to the fact that more stones were erected there. That more stones survived or were found there, and the seemingly uneven spread of their locations across the region could also be due to the fact that borders between the countries have changed over time, making some that would have originated in Denmark ending up in Sweden as we know it today.

Wherever they were originally created, it's amazing that so many runestones are still in existence, as they provide a fascinating insight into the life, mythology, folklore and customs of previous generations.

Many runestones were used as a means to commemorate the dead, much as memorials are today, and were often positioned near to where people died, although not necessarily at the actual site of their grave. Some stones were seemingly used to record descriptions of battles, mark territory, share heroic acts, explain inheritance, share significant events and folklore tales, or even to record curses.

Runestones often include the name of the person who raised the stone or wrote the inscription, along with other family members, as well as including the name of the actual person the stone commemorates. Such information offers insight into the various families and clans. There are several notable runestones in Sweden, for example, that feature the same names and same unique style of runic writing – even though one stone is a considerable distance from the others – which has led historians to believe they are all linked to the same clan.

Due to their age and if there are no clues given in the inscriptions, it can be hard to precisely date some individual runestones. However, it is possible for historians to roughly estimate their likely placement. The style of the carvings and type of runic alphabet used also helps provide guidelines as to the likely date of individual pieces.

Runes have appeared on many non-stone items too, with inscriptions often added to metalwork items, including swords, knives and other battle paraphernalia. Sometimes runes were carved into bones to make amulets or keepsakes, and into wood including

Fragment of Viking Runestone in Stockholm, Sweden. It is 'Uppland Runic Inscription 53' and the writing says Torsten and Frogunn had the stone erected after their son.

the so-called 'training sticks' that helped people learn the runic symbols.

Ancient runestones have inspired many artists and creatives over the years. Did you know, for example, that some of the runic symbols found on the Rök runestone in central Sweden inspired the design of the 1990 album cover for *Tyr* by Black Sabbath? Ancient runes are more deeply embedded in today's world than you may realize. More ubiquitously, the logo for Bluetooth technology is formed from a combination of two runes that represented the initials of 10th-century king Harald of Denmark – H and B for Harald Bluetooth, his nickname.

Anundshög tumulus ancient burial ground near Västerås in Västmanland, Sweden.

Detail from one of the most famous rock carvings from the Viking era, the so-called Sigurd carving neaby lake Malaren in Sweden.

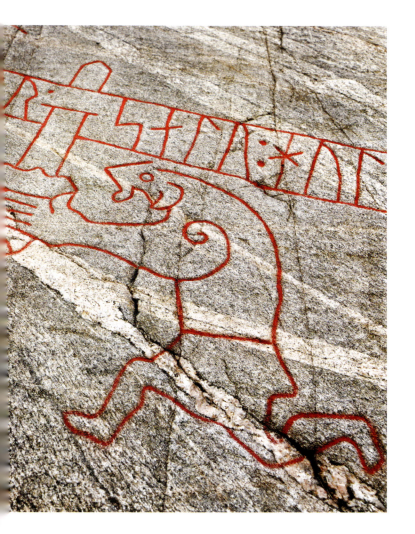

133

Lingsberg Runestones, Sweden

At a farm in Lingsberg, near Vallentuna in Sweden, two ancient runestones, together with one smaller fragmented stone, were found during work on the land in a valley called Angarnsjöängen. It was previously a very marshy area, but was drained in the late 19th century.

Known as Lingsbergsstenen 1 and Lingsbergsstenen 2, the two main stones were clearly inscribed to commemorate members of the same family and were initially placed facing each other as a tribute.

Lingsbergsstenen 1 is a large vertically erected and beautifully designed stone. It features runic text written in Younger Futhark that runs around the outside of the stone to form a border. It's interesting to note the mix of style influences involved in the design of the stone. In the centre there were artistic representations of serpents – also known as lindworms – various animals and a Celtic-style cross.

When translated into Norse the transcription on the stone reads:

'Dan ok Huskarl ok Svæinn ok Holmfriðr, þaun møðgin letu retta stæin þenna æftiʀ Halfdan, faður þæiʀa Dans, ok Holmfriðr at boanda sinn.'

When translated into English, it's thought to read:

'Danr and Húskarl and Sveinn and Holmfríðr, the mother and (her) sons, had this stone erected in memory of Halfdan, the father of Danr and his brothers; and Holmfríðr in memory of her husbandman.'

Lingsbergsstenen 1 runestone found at a farm in Lingsberg, near Vallentuna in Sweden.

135

Lingsberg Runestones, Sweden
(continued)

The second stone, Lingsbergsstenen 2, was discovered when a field was being ploughed. It has since been moved, but remains on the site of the farm in Lingsberg. The design on this runestone featured an intricate serpent winding around the stone, with the runic inscription carved into it. Again, there was a small cross included at the top, highlighting a mix of Christian and other influences.

When translated into Norse the inscription reads:

'En Dan ok Huskarl ok Svæinn letu retta stæin æftiʀ Ulfrik, faðurfaður sinn. Hann hafði a Ænglandi tu giald takit. Guð hialpi þæiʀa fæðga salu ok Guðs moðiʀ.'

This translates in English to:

'And Danr and Húskarl and Sveinn had the stone erected in memory of Ulfríkr, their father's father. He had taken two payments in England. May God and God's mother help the souls of the father and son.'

The inscription reveals that Ulfríkr had taken two payments in England, which are likely to have been danegelds, a type of Danish tax that Viking raiders paid in order to prevent land from being destroyed. This is a useful piece of information, as it helps date the runestones to around the 11th century, when danegelds were common.

The smaller fragment of stone did have some runic inscriptions on it, but sadly they are barely readable now. The stone remains on the land in Lingsberg and has been positioned next to Lingsbergsstenen 2.

Lingsbergsstenen 2 runestone featuring an intricate serpent design and runic inscription.

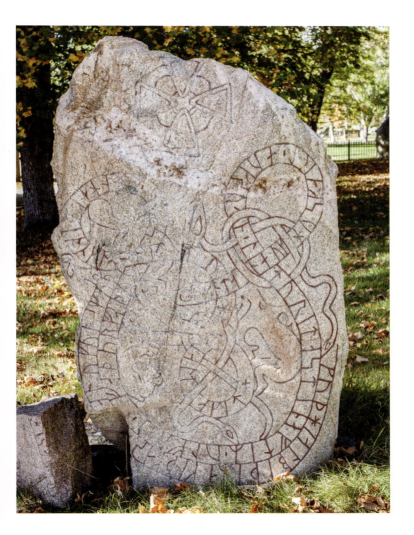

Möjbro Runestone, Sweden

The Möjbro Runestone was found, not surprisingly, in Möjbro, in Uppsala County, Sweden, and is believed to have first been discovered in the 1600s. Its exact original location is sadly unknown, but this magnificent runestone is historically significant for several reasons.

Measuring 2.46m (8ft 1in) in height, the Möjbro Runestone is made of granite and is inscribed in ancient Norse using the Elder Futhark runic symbols. It was originally thought to have dated to as far back as the 3rd century, but more recent estimates place it as likely to date from the 5th or 6th century.

As well as the rune inscriptions, the stone depicts a nicely carved image of a horse with a rider and two dogs following alongside. The image had survived well and was still relatively clear when details of the stone were first recorded. The style of imagery has been likened to Germanic images of horse-riding warriors and indicates that the runestone could well have been placed in memory of someone who had gone to war and not returned.

It's rare to find runestones inscribed in the ancient Norse language (also known as Proto-Norse) and especially featuring Elder Futhark runes, so the stone was, and remains, an exciting discovery.

The inscription on the stone has to be read from right to left, and from the bottom to the top, which has posed tricky for people to read. However, the inscription is believed to read: 'Frawarādaz ainahāhæislaikinaz.'

There have been many translations and attempts to interpret this runic inscription. It is most likely that Frawarādaz is the name of the person for whom the stone commemorates and that he died (part of the wording towards the end may be 'slaginaz', which translates as 'slain.'). The exact translation of the parts in between is unclear, but it's likely to refer to characteristics of the person being remembered, or what he was doing before he lost his life.

Although the runestone is made of granite, which is a stone renowned for its strength and durability, it had naturally become weathered from years of existence and exposure to the unpredictable outdoor elements. The runic inscription and artwork had largely survived well, but the stone itself was gradually becoming more and more fragile.

Möjbro Runestone in Sweden, which has a runic inscription and a carved image of a horse and rider.

In order to protect it from any further damage or wear and to retain it for future generations, the decision was therefore made in 1948 to move the stone from its location in Möjbro to a new home. It can now be found at the Swedish Museum of National Antiquities where it has been historically preserved.

Kylver Stone, Sweden

Many runestones have acquired their names due to where they were located, and the Kylver Stone is no exception. In 1903, an old cemetery near a farm at Kylver in the province of Gotland in Sweden was being excavated when this runestone was unexpectedly found. The stone had previously gone unnoticed as it had been used to seal a tomb and the runic inscription was hidden underneath it. The stone is thought to date from the 5th century.

The stone was a large, flat heavy limestone slab and it intrigued its discoverers because, rather than having a standard inscription on it commemorating a person, it instead had all of the runes from the Elder Futhark written on it. In addition, there was an extra rune that looked a bit like a very twiggy tree, but could potentially have been the rune Tiwaz, plus the addition of the word 'sueus.'

Speculation has been rife over the years as to the significance of the carved runic symbols on the Kylver Stone. One theory suggests that the inclusion of all the runes could have been a form of protection for the person whose body was buried in the tomb, particularly as the stone was placed facing the coffin. The use of the word 'sueus', which is palindromic, could indicate a ritual to bring extra protection.

Others suggest that the inclusion of the extra symbol at the end of the Elder Futhark could represent a bindrune. This is a form of runic symbol used for magical purposes and, in this case, could be several Tiwaz runes, or even a mix of the Tiwaz and Ansuz runes put together for maximum effect.

Both Tiwaz and Ansuz are relevant runic symbols for a gravestone. Tiwaz was the first rune in Tyr's Aett and represents the god Tyr, while Ansuz also means god and may signify Odin. Used in this context, they could be placed to ask the gods to give protection and courage to the spirit of the dead person.

Some theories suggest that the stone could have simply been used to cover the tomb because it was readily available. It may have been used by someone who was practising inscribing the runes – similar to the way in which we learn to write the alphabet at school – and they just happened to be on the reverse of the stone when it was reused to cover a grave.

Whatever the original purpose, the fact remains that the Kylver Stone

Runic inscription on the Kylver Stone found near a farm in Gotland, Sweden.

features one of the oldest known sequential examples of written Elder Futhark runes and is a historically significant find. The stone can now be found in the Swedish History Museum in Stockholm.

Stenkvista Runestone, Sweden

Popular images from Norse mythology often appear alongside inscriptions on stones, as is the case with the Stenkvista Runestone. This stone is located near the Stenkvista church in Södermanland County in south-east Sweden. The vertical standing runestone is made from granite and measures approximately 2.2m (7.2ft)high. The Swedish National Heritage Board hold a record of ancient runestones and images show that, although the runestone is in Stenkvista, it has been moved from its original location. According to the translation of the inscription, the runestone was placed by three siblings as a memorial to their father.

The design on this runestone isn't artistically outstanding, but it clearly helped to personalize the stone when it was created. It features a border running around the outside, in which most of the runic inscription was carved. At the bottom of the stone, the border design is finished off in the corners with swirly snakes and animal heads.

In the middle of the stone and coming down from the top border, there's a large image depicting Thor's hammer, or the Mjǫllnir (pronounced MIOL-neer). In Norse mythology, Thor was known as the god of thunder and his weapon was famously the Mjǫllnir. Although it's a weapon that could be used for destruction, the hammer also became associated with protection and was widely used in birth, marriage, death and burial ceremonies as a symbol of faith and blessing.

Depicted as it is here, on a memorial stone, it's likely that Thor's hammer was added as a symbol of consecration and protection, in a similar way to a cross being added to a Christian memorial. Amulets depicting Thor's hammer also became popular to wear, just like crosses.

Underneath the image of Thor's hammer is the name of the person for whom the stone was raised – Þjóðmundr – and the final two words, 'fôður sinn' meaning, 'their father'. When translated into English, the full inscription is believed to read:

'Helgi and Freygeirr and Þorgautr raised the rune-decorated landmark in memory of Þjóðmundr, their father'.

One aspect of the stone that has interested researchers is that the names of two Norse gods have been added to the names of the sons mentioned in the inscription. This practice is known as theophoric and describes the notion

Striking granite Stenvista Runestone in Södermanland County, southeast Sweden, located near the church.

of embedding the name of a god into a person's name.

In this instance, Germanic theophoric names have been used. For example, 'Freygeirr' has the name of the god Frey(r) included in it and 'Þorgautr' contains the name of the god Thor. The two names translate to mean, 'Freyr's Spear' and 'Thor-Goth'. It'a possible that they were used in this way to suggest that the names represent the characteristics of the individual sons.

Björketorp Runestone, Sweden

One of Sweden's most intriguing runestones can be found standing in a forest glade in Blekinge, near Ronneby. It's one of three menhirs – tall, vertical standing stones that form a triangular shape – and is notably one of the tallest runestones in the world, measuring about 4.2m (13.7ft) in height. Nearby, further into the forest, there's a small stone circle consisting of seven low stones.

Out of the three menhirs in the glade, only the Björketorp Runestone is inscribed (the other two are left blank) and its inscription is unusual in that it's not been made to remember a specific person.

The inscription is believed to date from about the 7th century and it's carved in a mix of Elder Futhark and Younger Futhark runes. This mix of runic alphabets can be seen on several other runestones, including more in Sweden, and may have been part of a local tradition used during this period.

The inscription on the granite stone is in two parts, with one part on the front of the stone, and one on the back. The inscription reads:

'Haidz runo runu, falh'k hedra ginnarunaz. Argiu hermalausz, ... weladauþe, saz þat brytz.

Uþarba spa.'

When translated into English, there are some variations on what this actually means. One version is:

'I, master of the runes(?) conceal here runes of power. Incessantly (plagued by) maleficence, (doomed to) insidious death (is) he who breaks this (monument).

I prophesy destruction / I predict perdition.'

However, the information board located at the site itself says:

'The series of honourable runes hid here, mighty runes. Restless of argiu (sexually submissive male), death by cunning, whom breaks it.

I predict ruin.'

The exact purpose of the Björketorp Runestone has been the subject

Opposite: The famous Björketorp Runestone, which stands vertically in a forest.

Björketorp Runestone, Sweden
(continued)

of much debate over the years. It was originally suggested that it had been placed on a grave, with the curse intended to protect it. However, an archaeological dig in 1914 uncovered no signs of any graves within the vicinity.

Other theories include the idea that it could have been erected as a memorial for someone who was buried elsewhere or that it could have served as a border marker between Sweden and Denmark, as the border line was previously nearby. Others have suggested it could have been used to mark a form of fertility shrine.

Interestingly, the Björketorp Runestone is thought to be related to the Stentoften, Istaby and Gunmarp runestones, all of which are also found in Sweden. Theories suggest that they were perhaps erected by the same clan, as they all carry the same mixed version of runic inscriptions; plus, some of them are linked by similar name inscriptions and curses.

Opposite: The Björketorp Runestone is one of the tallest runestones and is said to carry a curse.

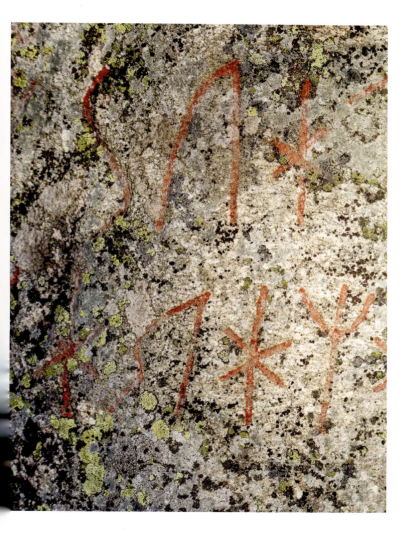

Björketorp runestone,
Johannishusåsen,
near Ronneby,
Blekinge, Sweden

Stentoften Runestone, Sweden

The Stentoften Runestone was discovered in 1823 in Stentoften, near Blekinge. When it was first found, it was lying face down and the runic inscription wasn't visible until it was moved. One aspect that intrigued archaeologists is that the runestone was surrounded by stones that formed a five-sided pentagram shape around it.

Pentagrams are widely associated with magic and witchcraft and, when the runestone was turned, it revealed an interesting inscription involving a spell or curse. The stone is believed to date from around the 7th century and it was inscribed with a mixture of the Elder Futhark and Younger or Scandinavian Futhark runes.

Although the stones are unlikely to have been carved by the same people, it may represent a runic tradition used by clans in the area during that particular period.

In Proto-Norse the inscription reads:

'<niuha>borumz <niuha>gestumz Haþuwulfz gaf j[ar], Hariwulfz ... ... haidiz runono, felh eka hedra niu habrumz, niu hangistumz Haþuwulfz gaf j[ar], Hariwulfz ... ... haidiz runono, felh eka hedra ginnurunoz. Hermalausaz argiu, Weladauþs, sa þat briutiþ.'

According to the Rundata project – a database of Nordic runic inscriptions – the English translation is:

'(To the) <niuha>dwellers (and) <niuha>guests Haþuwulfar gave ful year, Hariwulfar ... ... I, master of the runes(?) conceal here, nine bucks, nine stallions, Haþuwulfar gave fruitful year, Hariwulfar ... ... I, master of the runes(?) conceal here, runes of power. Incessantly (plagued by) maleficence, (doomed to) insidious death (is) he who this breaks.'

Like the Björketorp Runestone, the stone's inscription at Stentoften contains a curse or spell formula and it's one of the longest examples found on a runestone. Some suggest that it could represent a sacrifice made to the gods as part of a fertility ritual in the hope of receiving a bountiful harvest in return.

It's likely that Haþuwulfar and Hariwulfar are names, possibly of leaders or clan chieftains. The same names appear on the inscription on the Istaby Runestone, which was also found in the Blekinge area

Stentoften Runestone that was originally found near Blekinge in Sweden. The inscription contains a curse or spell.

of Sweden, reinforcing the idea that the stones were linked in some way. The names translate to mean 'battle wolf' and 'warrior wolf', suggesting that some form of wolf symbolism was important to the clan.

In 1864, the decision was made to move the Stentoften Runestone and it can now be found inside the porch of the Nikolai Church at Sölvesborg, in Blekinge County. It's a fitting location for an ancient runestone as the 13th-century church itself is rich with history too. Another runestone can also be found in front of the porch, with a Futhark inscription; it came from the ruins of the former Carmelite convent located next to the church.

Skanela Church, Sweden. There are fifteen runestones located in and in the close vicinity of the church.

Istaby Runestone, Sweden

The Istaby Runestone was discovered in about 1746 in the Istaby area of Blekinge and is a granite runestone with a runic inscription on either side. The vertical stone with its Proto-Norse Germanic inscription is believed to have been placed between the 6th and 8th centuries. Like some of the other stones found in the Blekinge region, such as the Stentoften, Björketorp and Gummarp runestones, the inscription on the Istaby stone is written in a runic style that combines the Elder Futhark and Younger or Scandinavian Futhark runes, and carries similar names. Due to the style of the runic writing, archaeologists believe the Istaby Runestone could be the oldest of these stones.

Unlike the Björketorp stone, which carried no names and didn't appear to be a memorial to an individual, the Istaby stone clearly was placed for memorial purposes. The inscription was written vertically down the length of the stone and on the side of it and, due to the lack of punctuation used with the runic alphabet, took a while to be transcribed, as it's hard to see where one word starts and ends.

However, experts did manage it and the inscription on the stone is believed to say:

'Aftr Hariwulfa. Haþuwulfz Heruwulfiz
Haþuwulfz Heruwulfiz aftr Hariwulfa
wrait runaz þaiaz.'

In English, this runestone transcription translates to mean:

"In memory of Hariwulfar. Haþuwulfar, Heruwulfar's son,
Haþuwulf(a)r, Heruwulfar's son, in memory of Hariwulfar
wrote these runes.'

As you can see, by the time it's transcribed, it's a somewhat simplistic inscription, even though the actual runic symbols took up a lot of space on the stone itself.

It was clearly written for memorial purposes and features people's names. Interestingly, it includes some of the same names that appeared on the Stentoften Runestone, which are thought to represent leaders or clan chieftains.

In English, the names translate to mean 'battle wolf', 'warrior wolf' and 'sword wolf', which suggests that the symbol of the wolf was significant to this particular clan and that perhaps they named each warrior after a wolf when they joined. Some suggest that the stone could have been raised to

The Istaby Runestone, on display in the Museum of National Antiquities in Stockholm.

remember important warriors from their tribe that never returned from battles.

The runestone, which was in good, complete condition considering its age, was moved from its original location and can now be found in the Museum of National Antiquities in Stockholm.

Gummarp Runestone, Sweden

The Gummarp Runestone was discovered in about 1627 in the village of Gummarp, in the Blekinge region of Sweden. Like the Stentoften, Istaby and Björketorp runestones, it's believed to date from between the 6th and 8th centuries and it shares similarities with these stones. In particular, like the other stones found in the area, the runic inscription on the Gummarp stone was written in the same unusual blend of Elder Futhark and Younger or Scandinavian runes. It's likely the stone and its inscription were created in the same era as the other stones too, as it contained similar wording.

Sadly, the Gummarp Runestone no longer exists. It was removed from its original location and taken to Copenhagen, where it was lost in the great Copenhagen fire of 1728 that destroyed approximately 28 per cent of the city. Thankfully, reproductions of the stone had been made for illustrative purposes, thus enabling the runic inscription to be recorded and analyzed over the years.

In Proto-Norse, the inscription reads:
'HaþuwulfR/HaþuwulfaR satte staba þria fff.'
In English, this is believed to translate to:
'Haþuwulfar placed three staves fff.'
Some interpretations suggest that there may have been another intended word at the beginning of the inscription, so it could have said, 'In memory of Haþuwulfar... placed [these] three staves fff.' This would make more sense if the stone had been placed for memorial purposes.

Either way, the use of 'fff' at the end of the inscription is likely to be three Fehu rune images, which look a bit like the letter 'f'. Fehu can be a symbol of wealth, so perhaps the writer was either declaring that Haþuwulfar had been wealthy or prosperous in life, or that they were adding the runic symbols to give him a prosperous send off to the afterlife.

The mention of 'placed three staves' could have figuratively referred to the addition of the three Fehu symbols, or related to a ritualistic offering that had been made as well.

Like the Stentoften and Istaby runestones, the Gummarp stone mentions the name Haþuwulfar ('battle wolf'), increasing the likelihood that these were significant members or leaders of a Germanic tribe in the area. It has fascinated historians that these three stones – along with the Björketorp

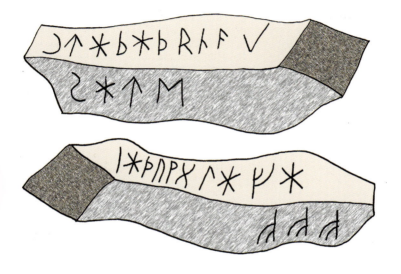

in a blend of Elder Futhark and Younger or Scandinavian runes.

Runestone – were all discovered intact within the same region of Sweden (even though the Björketorp stone was a considerable distance from the others) and are clearly linked to the same clan. Whether the practice of inscribing runestones with clan wolf-related names was unique, or whether other clans followed similar practices, is a mystery that only future runestone finds can reveal.

Rök Runestone, Sweden

The Rök Runestone (known in Sweden as Rökstenen) is one of Sweden's most famous runestones. As well as being huge in size – the stone measures about 2.4m (8ft) in height and weighs about five tonnes – it also features one of the longest known runic inscriptions in the world.

The massive stone has five sides, every one of which is covered in runic inscriptions. In fact, there are 28 lines of runes on the stone, totalling around 760 individual runic symbols. Whoever inscribed the stone did meticulous and sterling work, not least because it has survived so well.

Amazingly, this runestone has survived despite being used as a piece of building material. It was discovered during the 19th century built into the wall of a 12th-century church in Rök (hence its name). It was a common practice for builders of that time to use any materials they could get their hands on, so the runestone was recycled to become part of the building. Only a small amount of the stone was damaged in the process. The stone was removed from the building's walls oin 1862 and has been re-positioned under a protective shelter outside in the churchyard so that visitors can view it in all its glory.

It's likely that the inscription was carved onto the stone in the early 9th century and it's written partly in Elder Futhark and partly in Younger or Scandinavian Futhark runes. One aspect that's made the inscription tricky to decipher is that the carver used a mix of runic alphabets and appears to have added a few unique runes and riddles. These so-called cipher or code runes may have been a way of encrypting part of the inscription or could even signify that it was created as part of a magic ritual.

Not surprisingly, interpreting the true meaning of the inscription hasn't proved straightforward and there have been numerous theories about its meaning proposed over the years. Part of it is clearly a memorial; it translates into English as, 'In memory of Vámóðr stand these runes. And Varinn coloured them, the father, in memory of his dead son.'

It goes on to mention several Norse gods, including Thor, and folklore tales, in lines such as this that translate to read, 'I say the folktale / to the young men, which the two war-booties were, which twelve times were taken as war-booty, both together from various men.'

Some interpretations suggest the whole stone simply contains

Close up detail of part of the lengthy runic inscription on the Rök Runestone, or Rökstenen, one of Sweden's most famous runestones.

inscriptions involving a mix of folklore and stories of battles and heroic acts relating to Varinn and his tribe. Others that it was written as an offering for the gods. However, it begs the question as to why the carver went to the trouble of including riddles and ciphers? More recently, researchers have proposed an alternative interpretation suggesting that the inscription is linked to Norse mythology and involves the conflict between life and death and a possible climate crisis. Whatever its original meaning, the fact remains that the Rök Runestone is a truly magnificent ancient stone and a masterpiece of runic writing.

Jelling Stones, Denmark

The Jelling Stones are two of the most significant runestones in Denmark and date from the 10th century. Located in the town of Jelling in southern Denmark, the stones were raised by royalty and stand side by side outside the church. The first of the stones was erected by King Gorm the Old, in memory of his wife Thyra.

The runic inscription on Gorm's stone – the older and smaller runestone – is written vertically in three lines on one side, and a single line on the other side. According to the National Museum of Denmark, in Old Norse the transcription reads: 'Gormr konungr gerði kumbl þessi ept Þyri konu sína, Denmarkar bót.'

In English this translates to: 'King Gorm made these runes in honour of his wife Thyra, the pride of Denmark.'

The second stone, which is bigger in size and three-sided, was put there by King Harald, Gorm's son (also known as Harald Bluetooth). It was placed in memory of his parents, but also to boast about his conquest of Denmark and Norway and the fact that he had allegedly converted the Danes from Norse paganism to Christianity. In Norse the inscription reads:

'Haraldr konungr bað gǫrva kumbl þausi aft Gorm faður sinn auk aft Þórví móður sína. Sá Haraldr es sér vann Danmǫrk alla auk Norveg auk dani gærði kristna.'

In English this translates to:

'King Harald ordered these kumbls made in memory of Gorm, his father, and in memory of Thyra, his mother; that Harald who won for himself all of Denmark and Norway and made the Danes Christian.'

King Harald had been raised by his parents as a pagan, but in about the 960s, he converted to Christianity and was baptized. Passionate about his new faith, he commanded his subjects to become Christians too, and even went to the trouble of exhuming the bodies of his parents and giving them a Christian burial, despite them having been wholeheartedly pagan. It was at this point that the second Jelling stone was installed.

One of the 10th century Jelling Stones. This one was raised by King Gorm the Old in the town of Jelling, southern Denmark.

Second Jelling Stone, erected by King Harald in memory of his parents.

Jelling Stones, Denmark
(continued)

Compared to the first Jelling stone, the second is far more detailed. It was originally painted in bright colours and features an interesting mix of styles. The inscriptions were written in the runic alphabet and one side has an image of a lion with a serpent wrapped around it, which is likely to represent King Harald's battle and conquest.

The other side of the stone features one of the earliest known images from Denmark of Jesus Christ. It shows a figure with arms outstretched in a cross shape, a halo above their head, with vines or branches binding their arms.

Due to their position outside the church, the stones have been exposed to the elements for thousands of years. Considering their historical significance and importance in Danish history (the are affectionately known as 'Denmark's birth certificate'), they have now had specially constructed protective glass cases placed around them.

The two runestones, along with burial mounds and the church at Jelling, are on the UNESCO World Heritage List. A coloured replica of the stone can be found at the National Museum of Denmark in Copenhagen.

Ålum Runestones, Denmark

The Ålum Runestones are a collection of four stones that are located outside and inside the village church at Ålum, near Randers in Denmark.

The stone known as Ålum 1 was found in 1843, broken into three pieces and used as building material in the corner of the church porch. It was common practice in the past for pieces of stone to be recycled and reused in this way, especially before the historical significance of runestone inscriptions became apparent, but sadly it did result in part of the original stone being missing.

The pieces were removed from the building in 1879 and re-constructed to try and reveal the runic inscription. It was written in Elder Futhark runes and turned out to be a memorial.

In Old Norse, the visible parts of the inscription are believed to say: 'Toli res[þ]i sten þæssi æft Ingiald, sun sin, miok go[þan dræn]g. Þø munu minni...'

In English, this translates to:

'Tóli raised this stone in memory of Ingialdr, his son, a very good valiant man. This memorial will…'

Ålum 2 was also found embedded in the church building in 1843, this time in the north-east foundation of the nave, and was removed in 1879. Sadly, this stone was badly damaged and the inscription proved difficult to read or translate. Ålum stones one and two can now both be found on display in the porch of the church.

The third Ålum runestone is 205cm (6.7ft) tall and was discovered in 1890, located at the bottom of the church hill. This stone was written in Younger or Scandinavian Futhark and the inscriptions are largely around the outside of the stone, as if following the outline shape. The other side of the stone has images carved into it, including a rider on a horse carrying a pole and shield.

In Old Norse, the inscription reads:

'Wigotr resþi sten þænsi æftiʀ Æsgi, sun sin. Guþ hialpi hans sælu wæl.'

In English, this is thought to translate to: 'Végautr raised this stone in memory of Ásgeirr, his son. May God well help his soul.'

One of the Ålum Runestones found at village church at Ålum, near Randers, Denmark.

Example of a runic inscription found on one of the Ålum Runestones in Denmark.

Ålum Runestones, Denmark
(continued)

This inscription has proved interesting to researchers, especially since it ends with a Christian reference. The use of the Norse word, 'sælu', which means 'soul' dates the stone to at least the 10th century, when the word first became used in Scandinavia. It also suggests that the stone was carved after the Jelling Stones were erected in Denmark, as it indicates that the father was Christian. This stone has moved from its original location and now stands in the church graveyard.

The final runestone, Ålum 4, is 150cm (5ft) tall and was found in 1902, in the dyke at the church cemetery. This stone is believed to have been inscribed by the same person who produced the inscription on Ålum 3 because it's also written in Younger Futhark runes and has a similar style.

In Old Norse, the inscription says:

'Þorwi, Wigots kona, let resa sten þænsi æftiʀ Þorbiorn, sun Sibbu, systling sin, æs hon hugþi bætr þan swasum syni.'

In English, this translates to:

'Þyrvé, Végautr's wife, had this stone raised in memory of Þorbjǫrn, son of Sibbi, her cousin, whom she cared for more than had he been her own son / than a dear son.'

Ålum 4 can now be found standing next to Ålum 3 in the church graveyard.

Mejlby Stone, Denmark

The Mejlby Stone is an inscribed runestone that was found in a pond in Mejlby, located about 20km (12mi) from the city of Randers in Denmark. It is believed to have originally been placed near a burial mound and is thought to date from the late 10th or early 11th century.

The tall vertical runestone was made from granite and inscribed using the Younger or Scandinavian Futhark runic alphabet. No images appeared on the stone, just three vertical rows of runes diligently carved into the stone and surrounded by simple rounded borders.

The stone was created by a father in memory of his son, who died in a shipwreck. In Old Norse the inscription reads:

'Áni reisti stein þenna ept Áskel, son sinn, er dauðr varð með Þóri í Eyrasundi.' When translated into English, it is believed to say:

'Áni raised this stone in memory of Áskell, his son, who died with Þórir in The Sound.'

The Mejlby Stone can now be found in the Cultural History Museum in Randers. Since 2009, the runestone has been part of an impressive interactive exhibition involving projected images, animation and sound to bring the runic writing to life. The installation tells visitors the story of Áni and his son Áskell who was sent on a journey that ended with him losing his life in a shipwreck in the Sound. The Mejlby Stone is one of five runestones held at the museum, which is a must-visit location for runestone fans.

The Mejlby Stone dates from the late 10th or early 11th century and was found in a pond in Mejlby, Denmark.

Old Runestones of Norway

Some runestone specimens are undoubtedly huge and impressive, but small examples can be beautiful too. The Barmen Runestone in Norway is an example of a small and ancient runestone that has been well preserved. In fact, it's one of the oldest examples of a stone with an Elder Futhark runic inscription and is believed to date to AD 300–450.

Barmen is a small island in Vestland County, Norway. The runestone itself is a single standing stone located close to the coastal road and facing the shore. It stands about 1.5m (5ft) high and 60cm (2ft) wide. The inscription – 'ekþirþijaʀru' – is carved vertically into the side of the stone and is believed to say: 'I, Þirbijaʀ, (carved? the) ru(ne/-s?)'. Another translation suggests 'I, Þirbijaʀ' means 'he that makes people powerless'. In this context, the inscription could have been a curse made by a clan leader staking his claim on the land.

Another old runestone is the Einang Stone, which is located near Fagernes in the Oppland region of Norway, and was discovered in 1938. Believed to date from about the 4th century, this stone also features an Elder Futhark inscription. It is thought to be one of the oldest surviving runestones still located in its original position, on a grave mound overlooking the Valdres valley. Due to its age and history, the Einang Stone has been protected by a small wooden and glass structure.

In Norse the inscription says: '(Ek go)ðagastiz runo faihido.'

In English, this translates to: '(I, Go)dguest inscribed the runes.'

The stone may have the earliest inscription that appears to be a memorial to not mention the name of the person who died and instead simply feature the name of the person who inscribed the stone, a fact that has led to much debate over the years. Did the carver intend to write more, but run out of steam before doing so?

The Einang Stone is located east of the Einang Sound near Fagernes, in Oppland, Norway.

The Einangsteinen inscription.

Dynna Stone, Norway

Whereas many memorial runestones tend to have been placed by fathers or men, the Dynna Stone differs in that the inscription tells us it was placed by a woman. The stone was found at the Nordre Dynna farm near Gran, Hadeland in Norway in 1823. The stone is about 3m (9.8ft) tall and is triangular in shape, with a wider base that tapers up to a point. It's made from a reddish brown-coloured sandstone and is thought to date from the 11th century.

The stone was originally located on the farmland, where it was believed to have been placed on a burial barrow. However, during the 1700s, it was moved into a barn where it was reportedly used as a rather elaborate salt lick for cows. In the 1800s it was moved back to its original position outside, but sadly by this point it had lost its tip and was at risk of further erosion. In 1879 it was acquired by the Museum of Cultural History in Oslo and moved there where it still remains. A replica of the stone can be found at Hadeland Folkemuseum in Gran.

Due to being outside and exposed to the elements, parts of the stone have been damaged. Small marks and holes dot the surface and someone had even carved their initials and a date into it in the 1800s. However, its runic inscription has remained clear, as has a panel of important pictorial images.

The runic inscription runs down one of the edges of the stone, written in the Younger or Scandinavian Futhark. There are some inconsistencies with the usual style of runes, with a mix of long-branch and short-twig runes used; this may be due to local customs or simply the style used by the inscriber.

In Norse, the inscription says:

'Gunnvǫr gerði brú, Þryðríks dóttir, eptir Ástríði, dóttur sína. Sú var mær hǫnnurst á Haðalandi.'

In English this tranlates to:

'Gunnvôr, Þryðríkr's daughter, made the bridge in memory of her daughter Ástríðr. She was the handiest maiden in Haðaland.'

The fact that Gunnvôr was able to build a bridge and have a runestone carved and erected highlights that she must have been a wealthy woman and an elite member of society. It provides a fascinating insight into the role of women in the Viking Age and one that's important as so often history depicts societies dominated by men. The reference to the daughter being the 'handiest maiden,' may relate to her being skilled at crafts and needlework.

Also on the stone is a panel of carved images running down one side. They're significant as they are believed to be among the earliest forms of Christian art found in Norway. Although crude in design, the images depict the nativity scene and the baby Jesus, as well as the the Star of Bethlehem and the arrival of the Three Wise Men on horseback. This is an indication that Christianity had reached the community and that the images were important enough to be used to create a memorial for a special daughter.

11th century Dynna Stone, found on farmland in 1823.

Alstad Runestone, Norway

In the same way that some runestones have been recycled as building materials, other stones have also been reused for inscriptions. This is the case with the Alstad Runestone, which was found at Alstad farm, Toten in Oppland. The red-brown sandstone runestone is approximately 2.7m (8.8ft) tall and features two runic inscriptions written in Younger or Scandinavian Futhark – one of which is believed to be older than the second – plus some carved pictorial images.

The stone originally stood upright outside the Alstad farmhouse, but in the 19th century it was damaged by something falling on it. It ended up lying horizontally on the ground for some time after, before being hoisted back into an upright position. Naturally, the stone has been affected by age and exposure to weather, plus there are several small holes on its surface (possibly from being hit by arrow shots) and signs that weapons may have been sharpened on the stone in the past.

Three sides of the stone are covered in runic inscriptions and carved imagery. The longest and oldest inscription runs vertically from the bottom to the top of the narrow side of the stone and continues on one of the carved sides.

In Old Norse the inscription reads:

'Jórunnr reisti stein þenna eptir ⟨au-aun-⟩ er hana [á]tti, ok fœrði af Hringaríki útan ór Ulfeyj[u].

Ok myndasteinn [mæt]ir þessi.'

In English this translates to:

'Jórunnr raised this stone in memory of who owned her, and (she) brought (it) out of Hringaríki, from Ulfey.

And the picture-stone venerates them.'

The reference to the person 'who owned her', is likely to be her husband.

The two broad sides of the stone both feature carvings. On one side, it's filled with decorative ornate scrollwork-style designs. On the other side, at the top there's a carved bird – likely an eagle – then various images of horses, some with riders who appear to be going into battle, running down the vertical length.

The additional inscription that was added approximately 50–70 years later in the early part of the 11th century, has been squeezed onto the same side that features the carved animals, sitting in three horizontal lines underneath the images.

In Old Norse it reads:

'Engli reisti stein þenna eptir Þórald, son sinn, er varð dauðr í Vitaholmi, miðli Vitaholms ok Garða.'

In English this translates to:

'Engli raised this stone in memory of Þóraldr, his son, who died in Vitaholm – between Vitaholm and Garðar.' Vitaholm is thought to be the old name for Kiev in Ukraine and Gardar was the name previously used for Russia. In 1913, the stone moved to the collection at the Museum of Cultural History in Oslo where it is on display alongside other notable runestones.

Alstad Runestone, Norway

Høre Stave Church, Norway

Høre is one of many medieval stave churches that were built in Norway from the 11th to the 13th centuries. They're known as stave churches due to the way they are constructed, using wooden timber posts and lintels called 'stafr' – or staves. The church, which is located in the village of Kvien in Vang, eastern Norway, is believed to date to at least 1179, thanks to information from the runic inscriptions found in the church and dendrochronology (tree-ring dating) that has been carried out to date the wood. It's likely that an older structure may have been on the site previously, as a coin dating from about 1100 was found under the floor.

There are several runic inscriptions in the church, including one important one on the pulpit that helped to date the building. In Old Norse it reads:

'Þá, um þat sumar [létu] þeir brœðr Erlingr ok Auðun hôggva till kirkju þessar, er Erlingr ja[rl fe]ll í Niðarósi.'

In English it translates to:

'The brothers Erling and Audun had the timber for this church felled, the summer that Earl Erling fell in Nidaros.'

The inscription makes reference to the Battle of Kalvskinnet in Nidaros (present-day Trondheim), which took place in 1179 and where Earl Erling Skavve was known to have fallen.

Although the church has been redeveloped over the years, the original construction of the nave from the 12th century remains and helps provide an indication of the original size of the building.

Many runic inscriptions in Norway were found in stave churches. Other notable inscriptions have been found in Hegge Stave Church, Borgund Stave Church and Lo Stave Church, for example – but as archaeological digs expanded, items with runic inscriptions also began to be discovered in populated towns.

These inscriptions, affectionately known as Town Runes, tend to date between 1100–1300 and they provide a fascinating insight into how runes were used more widely as a form of written communication in Norway. Reading and writing runes wasn't taught in schools, so it seems likely that skills were passed down in families, from one generation to the next. Archaeological digs have discovered so-called 'training sticks' that were used to learn runes. The runes were carved into the sticks to help teach the meaning of each symbol, then other sticks were used by novices carving the symbols themselves.

The inscriptions that have been found in towns, such as Bryggen in Bergen, reveal that runes were typically used for the purpose of trading and conducting business. Inscriptions have been found relating to the purchase of goods including fish, grain, salt and beer.

Although most of the runic inscriptions were relatively short, one longer message was found carved onto a piece of wood. It appears to be written by a trader who may have been on an assignment, but has had difficulty in obtaining the goods he sought. In English the inscription translates to:

'To Havgrim, his companion, Tore the beautiful sends God's and his own greetings, true comradeship and friendship. I lack a lot of things, companion! Beer is not at hand, nor fish. I want you to know, but require nothing of me. Ask the farmer to come south to us and see how we are doing. Urge him to it and require nothing of me; and do not let Torstein the long know. Send me some gloves. If Sigrid needs anything, then offer it to her. Promise not to beat me because of my helplessness.'

The medieval Høre Stave Church in Norway, which has several notable runic inscriptions in the building.

Close-up of some of the ancient decorative elements found on the door of Høre Stave Church in Norway.

The Englandsstenarna

The so-called Englandsstenarna (or England runestones) refer to stones relating to England that have been discovered in northern Europe. There are around 30 or so known Englandsstenarna dotted around the region, including in Sweden and Denmark. The purpose of the runestones differed, but in some cases they related to Scandinavians who had travelled for migration, trade, battle or monetary purposes.

In the late 10th and early 11th centuries, Anglo-Saxon rulers paid danegelds – a form of tax to protect their land from attack – to Vikings who travelled to England. It was clearly a tempting way to make money, however, some Vikings never made it home, succumbing to death on the journey back or dying abroad.

In Grinda, Södermanland, Sweden a decorative and carved runestone was found standing in a field close to a road. The stone features two rows of runic inscriptions running around the outside of the stone, with decorative detail in the middle. It was placed in memory of a father who travelled to England to collect danegelds and fought towns in Germany.

In English the inscription said:

'Grjótgarðr (and) Einriði, the sons made (the stone) in memory of (their) able father. Guðvér was in the west; divided (up) payment in England; manfully attacked townships in Saxony.'

Another stone stands close to this one in Grinda, but it makes reference to a nephew who went to Greece to collect gold. Like the Englandsstenarna, there are a number of Greklandsstenarna (Greece runestones) that describe voyages made by the Norse to Greece.

At the church of Husby-Sjuhundra in Uppland, Sweden, there's a tall vertical runestone located outside the church in memory of a Viking who died in 1015. The inscription is written in one long, curved band going up and around the tall narrow shape of the stone. It tells of a trip to England that didn't go as planned.

In Old Norse the inscription says:

'Diarfʀ ok Orøkia ok Vigi ok Iogæiʀʀ ok Gæiʀhialmʀ, þæiʀ brøðr alliʀ letu ræisa stæin þenna æftiʀ Svæin, broður sinn. Saʀ varð dauðr a Iutlandi. Hann skuldi fara til Ænglands. Guð hialpi hans and ok salu ok Guðs moðiʀ bætr þan hann gærði til.'

Ancient Väsby runestone with a runic inscription running around the edge and images in the centre. Located in Värmdö near Stockholm.

Example of one of the ornate Lilla Vilunda runestones found in Stockholm County, Sweden.

The Englandsstenarna
(continued)

In English it translates to:

'Djarfr and Órœkja and Vígi and Jógeirr and Geirhjalmr, all of these brothers had this stone raised in memory of Sveinn, their brother. He died in Jútland. He meant to travel to England. May God and God's mother help his spirit and soul better than he deserved.'

Another church in Orkesta, also in Uppland, Sweden, has a runestone outside that was discovered in 1868 in Yttergärde. It is interesting because it describes not only one voyage to England for danegeld, but three – all made by the same person over a number of years.

In Old Norse, it says:

'En Ulfʀ hafiʀ a Ænglandi þry giald takit. Þet vas fyrsta þet's Tosti ga[l]t. Þa [galt] Þorkætill. Þa galt Knutr.'

In English it translates to:

'And Ulfr has taken three payments in England. That was the first that Tosti paid. Then Þorketill paid. Then Knútr paid.' Given the amount of payments Ulfr had received, he may well have lived a wealthy life in Sweden.

Bewcastle Cross, England

Standing in the churchyard of St Cuthbert's Church in Bewcastle in the English county of Cumbria, you'll find the Anglo-Saxon Bewcastle Cross. The cross, which is believed to date from the 7th or 8th century, is sadly no longer whole (the top is missing) but it still stands 4.4m (14.4ft) high and features a stunning array of carved decorations and runic inscriptions on it.

The four faces of the cross – north, south, east and west – are all beautifully carved, often with several different panels, and have designs that include animals, figures, knots, scrolls and chequers in addition to runes.

The carvings on the west side of the cross all feature biblical figures. At the top, John the Baptist is shown holding a lamb. In the middle there's an image of Christ with animals at his feet and at the bottom there's a figure of a man with a bird next to him. Some believe this third figure is St John the Evangelist, as he was often shown with an eagle, but the exact identity of this figure has been the subject of much debate because the style is unusual. There is a hole in the cross next to his arm, which may have been used to hold some form of religious relic.

One of the runic inscriptions resides between figures two and three on the west side of the cross, and there are others on the north face. Sadly, the runic inscriptions are relatively worn and the only name that has been fully deciphered is that of Cynnburug.

The stunning Anglo-Saxon Bewcastle Cross in the churchyard at St Cuthbert's in Bewcastle, Cumbria.

Ruthwell Cross, Scotland

Described as 'the cousin' of the Bewcastle Cross, the Ruthwell Cross is located in the village of Ruthwell in Dumfries and Galloway, Scotland. Like the Bewcastle Cross, it's unusual in that it features runic inscriptions on what is essentially a Christian cross.

The cross itself is thought to date from the 8th century and is regarded as one of the best examples of carved Anglo-Saxon work. Thankfully, it has been successfully pieced together since being damaged in 1642 and it shares similarities in design with the Bewcastle Cross.

The cross features multiple panels of carvings, depicting scenes from the New Testament, plus inscriptions in both Latin and runes. The images shown on the cross include Mary Magdalene, Martha and Mary, Mary and Joseph, St John the Evangelist as well as Jesus performing healing and miracles. There are also decorative panels of swirling vines and animals.

The runic inscription has been interepreted as being from an Old English poem *The Dream of the Rood*. The only other known copy of the poem text is the Vercelli Book, a manuscript dating from the 10th or early 11th century, which can be found in the library at Vercelli Cathedral in Italy.

However, scholars have suggested that the runic inscription was in fact added after the original creation of the cross because it doesn't match the usual memorial style that tended to be carved on stone and it dates from a period later than when the cross was originally made. One of the oldest works in English literature, the poem tells the story of the crucifixion from the perspective of the tree that was cut to make the cross.

The Ruthwell Cross is situated in Ruthwell Parish Church.

Maeshowe, Scotland

History collides at Maeshowe on the main island of Orkney, an archipelago in the Northern Isles of Scotland, where one of the finest chambered tombs in north-west Europe is also home to a number of runic inscriptions. The expansive Neolithic burial chamber is located about 500m (0.3mi) from Harray Loch. From the outside it simply looks like a large grassy mound, but there is actually a 10m (32ft)-long passageway leading inside that opens up into a central chamber, with upright standing stones in each corner, and areas leading off from it.

The burial chamber was first excavated in 1861 by a team led by the British antiquarian and MP, James Farrer. The team gained access by opening up a shaft through the top of the mound, which took them down into the cairn. Much to their surprise, they discovered that they weren't the only ones who had discovered the tomb – Vikings had been there previously.

Inside, the walls were covered in runic graffiti, from Vikings who'd found the tomb on their travels and used it as a convenient shelter from the elements. About 30 different runic inscriptions were discovered, making it one of the largest and most significant runic finds in Europe.

The main chamber alone had 24 runic inscriptions on the walls, as well as several other indistinguishable marks, together with three drawings that are thought to represent a walrus, a dragon and a serpent.

The content of the inscriptions themselves is mixed. Some of the statements are simply written in the style of graffiti as we would recognize it today, with individuals making their mark and declaring their presence.

For example:

'Haermund Hardaxe carved these runes.'

'Ottarfila carved these runes.'

'Tholfr Klossienn's son carved these runes high up.' The latter inscription was found high up on the wall.

'These runes were carved by the man most skilled in runes in the western ocean.'

'Arnfithr Matr carved these runes with this axe owned by Gauk.'

Other inscriptions were longer, telling tales, such as:

'It is surely true what I say that treasure was carried off in three nights before those... crusaders broke into this howe.' The word 'howe' means 'hill' in Old Norse.

'To the north-west is a great hidden treasure. It was long ago that a treasure was hidden here. Happy is he that might find that great treasure.'

Other than the odd name that has been included in the inscriptions, it's hard to be sure exactly which Vikings may have been in the burial chamber. Some ideas can be gleaned from the Orkneyinga saga (also known as the History of the Earls of Orkney and Jarls' Saga), a narrative text written in the late 12th and early 13th centuries by an unnamed Icelandic author.

According to the Orkneyinga saga, in 1153 a group of Viking warriors led by Earl Harald were said to have made their way from Stromness to Firth and took shelter in an ancient structure. Once inside, while waiting for bad weather to pass, they are said to have carved runic graffiti into the walls. If the tale is true, perhaps the inscriptions could have been the work of their hands? Strangely, none of the Neolithic skeletons believed to have originally been interred in the chamber were discovered and it's unclear when they were removed.

In addition to the Maeshowe runes, there are nearly 20 other documented runic finds in Orkney. For example, runic inscriptions can be seen on one of the standing stones at the Ring of Brodgar and a cairn at Unstan, both in the Stenness area.

Runic inscriptions and Viking graffiti found on the walls inside the Maeshowe neolithic burial chamber.

Maeshowe neolithic burial chamber located near Harray Loch in Maeshowe, Orkney.

Franks Casket, England

One of the most impressive artefacts featuring runic inscriptions is the Franks Casket, a lidded Anglo-Saxon casket made from whalebone. The box features intricate carvings all over it, including a mix of runic and Latin inscriptions. Franks Casket is believed to date from the 8th century and potentially originate from Northumbria. The rectangular casket measures approximately 22.9 x 19 x 10.9cm (9 x 7.5 x 5in) in size.

Franks Casket is regarded as one of the most important Anglo-Saxon artefacts and the decorated panels are a spectacular example of skill and workmanship. The casket has narrative imagery carved into it, featuring an eclectic mix of Germanic, Christian, Roman and Jewish traditions. Each panel is accompanied by text, written in runes and Latin.

Some of the inscriptions have proved difficult to translate, not least because there are adaptations or runic symbols and cryptic runes included, but they appear to tell tales and stories, rather like a book.

There's a runic riddle running along the front panel of the casket which, when translated, describes how and why whalebone came to be used to produce the casket:

'The flood cast up the fish on the mountain-cliff. The terror-king became sad where he swam on the shingle. Whale's bone.'

The image on the left front of the box is believed to show a scene from the Weland (Wayland) the Smith legend. This popular Germanic legend told the story of a flying blacksmith. The right side of the front panel shows the Adoration of the Magi and has the word 'mægi' carved around it.

The left-hand end panel has a carved image of Romulus and Rebus being nurtured by a wolf, and the inscription says:

'Romulus and Remus, two brothers, a she-wolf nourished them in Rome, far from their native land.'

The back panel of the casket has an image depicting the capture of Jerusalem by Titus, who later became emperor. The inscription reads:

'Here Titus and a Jew fight: here its inhabitants flee from Jerusalem.'

The right-hand end panel has proved tricky to translate as the runic text is partially cryptic, but it's believed to possibly say:

'Here Hos sits on the sorrow-mound; she suffers distress in that Ertae had decreed for her a wretched den of sorrows and torments of mind.'

The design on the lid of the casket is thought to relate to Egil, a Germanic hero. It has the word, 'aegili' carved on it.

Franks Casket is now in the British Museum in London, but it had a chequered history prior to being moved there. At one point it may have belonged to the Saint-Julien church in Brioude in France; then it was owned by a family in Auzon who used it as a sewing box. When the box fell apart, the parts were sold to a French antique shop where Sir Augustus Wollaston Franks bought it in 1857. Sensing the history of the piece, he donated it to the British Museum in 1867 and they repaid the favour by naming it after him.

Side panel of the Anglo-Saxon Franks Casket carved from the bone of a beached whale. From the British Museum's collection.

205

Runic Inscriptions from Vimose, Denmark

Archaeological excavations at Vimose, on the island of Funen in Denmark, have revealed a large collection of historical items, including several featuring Elder Futhark runic inscriptions. One of these – a comb – is believed to be one of the oldest Elder Futhark inscriptions ever found and has been dated to the 2nd or 3rd century. The comb is made from bone or horn, probably from an antler, and was discovered in 1865 in a bog in Vimose. The runic inscription consists of a single word, 'Harja.' Other items found in the same location with runic inscriptions on them include a buckle, a sheathplate, a spearhead, a woodplane and a chape (the metal point of a scabbard).

The inscriptions on some of these items haven't been fully translated, but the runes on the chape may say, 'Mari (the famous one) is the sword of Alla,' and on the sheathplate some of the words may say, 'son or descendant of Awa'.

Vimose is believed to be a sacrificial site, where items were thrown into the bog and sacrificed to the gods. It's possible that they were sacrificed in the hope of people receiving good luck and better harvests or as thanks to the gods for victory in battle.

As well as the items with runic inscriptions, many other sacrificial finds were discovered here from various historical periods, including weapons, pots, food and animals. Another comb with a runic inscription on it was found during archaeological excavations of a Viking Age marketplace in Ribe, one of Denmark's oldest towns. This piece was much younger than the Vimose comb, but was still regarded as an important find providing knowledge about Viking activity in the city.

The Ribe comb is thought to date from around the 9th century and it was found alongside a small piece of bone or antler that also featured a runic inscription on it. What interested archaeologists most was which runic alphabet they featured. It was about this time in history that the Elder Futhark started to peter out and the Younger or Scandinavian Futhark came into use. Archaeologists were previously unsure exactly where in Scandinavia the Younger Futhark first came into use. The theory was that it probably appeared in larger towns first, however, the discovery of the Ribe comb reveals that the community had already adopted the newer alphabet by the 9th century.

Simple Elder Futhark runic inscription found on a comb at Vimose, Denmark.

The markings on the comb were tricky to analyze, but it's thought to simply say, 'comb.' Interestingly, it says 'comb' on either side of the piece but is written slightly differently, so may have been inscribed by two different people.

Seax of Beagnoth, England
(Thames Scramasax)

Rivers and waterways frequently uncover ancient artefacts, and several pieces with runic inscriptions have been found over the years along the banks of the River Thames in London, England.

The Seax of Beagnoth, otherwise known as the Thames Scramasax, is a short single-edged sword that was found near Battersea in London in 1857. Dating from the late 9th or 10th century, the sword is decorated with inlaid copper, bronze and silver wire, along with geometric zigzag-style decoration, and has an interesting futhorc runic inscription along the length of its blade.

The first part of the inscription contains 28 letters of the Anglo-Saxon Futhorc. Separated by decoration is a second inscription containing the word 'bêagnoş'. The latter is believed

to be either the name of the sword owner, the person it was being gifted to or the blacksmith that made the piece.

Unusually, the futhorc runes aren't listed in their standard order – runes 20 to 23 were in the wrong order – and are carved strangely, with inconsistencies in their appearance.

The presence of these runes could purely have been for decorative purposes, but there's also the suggestion that they could have been added for magical purposes. However, it's odd that the futhorc alphabet has been carved incorrectly. Theories suggest that either the blacksmith copied them wrongly, that it could have been a local interpretation of the runes or that it was simply due to the technical difficulties of using inlaid wire to form runes on the sword.

The Seax of Beagnoth, a short single-edged sword found along the River Thames in London in 1857.

Undley Bracteate, England

In 1981 a farmer in Undley, Suffolk, discovered a gold bracteate, thought to date from the 5th century, when he was working in one of his fields. This find is not only stunning in appearance, but it is also highly significant for it features one of the earliest known runic inscriptions written in the Anglo-Frisian Futhorc. A bracteate is a thin gold medal that was worn as jewellery.

The small piece only measures 2.3cm (0.9in) in diameter, but is packed with intricate detail and design, including an image of a helmeted head, a wolf and a star. The runic inscription runs around the circumference of the piece, followed by a chevron-style border. It's thought that the inscription may read, 'howling she-wolf,' which would explain the inclusion of a wolf in the design.

Experts believe the bracteate is unlikely to have been made in England and was instead brought to the country from Scandinavia, especially as it has Scandinavian influences in the design. The Undley bracteate is now housed in the British Museum, London.

Gold bracteate pendant with an Anglo-Frisian runic inscription, found in Undley, Suffolk.

Thames Silver Mount, England

Another fine example of a runic artefact discovered in the River Thames is what has become known as the Thames Silver Mount. This object was found near Westminster Bridge in London in 1866, possibly as the result of dredging activities. Made of silver gilt, the fragmented mount would probably have been a sheath or scabbard fitting for a knife or small sword, like a seax. The shape of the object and the remnants of fittings on it suggests that it may have been fitted onto wood or leather.

Thought to date from the late 8th century, the silver mount was sadly broken when found but it still clearly displays an Anglo-Saxon Futhorc runic inscription along its remaining 18.8cm (7.4in) length. The runes appear to be:

The runic inscription on the Thames Silver Mount can be clearly seen here.

'sbe/rædht bcai | e/rh/ad/æbs'.

The inscription has unfortunately proved more difficult to interpret, but it's thought to have been placed specifically in that position so that it could be seen when the knife was being used. The runes may have been added for decoration or to serve a magical purpose, perhaps providing power or protection for the user.

In addition to the runes, the silver mount is decorated at one end with a distinctive open-mouthed animal head with sharp fangs, a curled tongue and eyes set with blue glass – a highly ornate and striking design.

Runic inscriptions found on items at Chessell Down, Isle of Wight, England

Archaeological digs at an Anglo-Saxon cemetery at Chessell Down on the Isle of Wight have revealed many items with Scandinavian links and runic inscriptions, suggesting a strong trading connection with the island.

One of the most intriguing items uncovered is a silver gilt scabbard mount, or sword sheath. Thought to date from the late 5th to early 6th century, the scabbard was designed to fit snugly on the blade of a sword. This particular piece is highly decorative and ornately made, featuring an openwork design, niello inlay and helmeted heads at either end.

On the back of the piece, silver strips were added at some point – possibly before the sword was buried – and a runic inscription was scratched onto it. The marks are quite faint, so the inscription was only discovered when it was being conserved at the British Museum in London.

The short inscription is written in Anglo-Saxon Futhorc runes and features seven characters, split into two groups. It may represent a name, but as there are slight variations in the design and style of the runes used, there is no consensus on the exact translation.

Although the scabbard with its runic inscription was possible the most stunning find at Chessell Down, other artefacts were found too, many of them buried in graves and with strong Scandinavian links. The Chessell Down pail, for example, was found buried in a woman's grave along with other items. The fact that she had items buried with her indicates that she was likely to have been wealthy or an important member of the community. The pail is Eastern Mediterranean in style and material with a runic inscription running around it.

While the inscription is hard to translate, what is interesting is that experts have suggested that the runes may have been added to the piece after it arrived in England. This suggests that early communities on the Isle of Wight may have used runes as part of their language and communication system. This ties in with the theory that the runes may have been added to the scabbard prior to it being buried and stresses the importance that runes may have held in the area at the time.

The Chessell Down sword sheath.

Loveden Hill Urn, England

Throughout history it's always been important to commemorate the dead, whether through burial stones, crosses or other items. One of the oldest Anglo-Saxon cemeteries was discovered at Loveden Hill in Lincolnshire. It was first excavated in the 1920s, then further digs occurred in the 1950s and 1970s. These revealed that the site covers approximately 1.2 acres (0.4 hectares) and is thought to date from the 5th to 7th centuries.

A number of significant items were found, including 1800 urns. One of the cremation urns, now known as the Loveden Hill urn, is thought to be one of the earliest pieces found in England with a runic inscription on it. Dating from the second half of the 5th century, the urn is made from clay and has runes cut into the side of the pot. The first part of the inscription says, 'sïþæbæd', which may be the name of the person whose remains are contained in the urn. It is followed by nine more runic letters, but the meaning of these remains unclear. What also intrigued archaeologists was that the clay used for this piece wasn't local to Lincolnshire, so it could have been brought to the site from elsewhere.

Caistor St. Edmund, England

One of the oldest items with a runic inscription thought to have been found in England is the Caistor St. Edmund (*Venta Icenorum*) or Caistor-by-Norwich Astragalus, which is believed to date from the 5th century. It was discovered in 1937 inside an urn in Caistor St Edmund in Norfolk. The astragalus is an ankle bone – in this case, thought to have been from a deer – and it has an Elder Futhark runic inscription carved on it. The inscription was simple, and said, 'raïhan' – which is believed to mean 'roe deer.'

Due to the nature of the object, theories suggest it could have originated in Scandinavia. It may have been brought over by Norse people migrating to England or brought back from Scandinavia as an early form of travel memento. It was interesting that it was found buried in an urn in a cemetery and must have had some kind of significance for the person whose ashes were stored there.

The Loveden Hill urn is believed to be one of the earliest known pieces found in England with a runic inscription on it.

Appendix: Elder Futhark Runes – Alternative Names

It's common to find variations in names for the runestones in the Elder Futhark. This is due in part to different spellings, dialect and interpretation. It can get confusing when you see the names spelled differently but, despite the wording, they are essentially the same stone with the same meanings.

Here's a useful guide to some of the alternative names of the 24 stones in the Elder Futhark that you may come across.

1. **Fehu** – Fuhu, Feh, Fe, Faihu, Frey
2. **Uruz** – Urox, Urus, Ur, Oruiox
3. **Thurisaz** – Thurs, Thursis, Thor
4. **Ansuz** – As, Aza, Oss, Ass
5. **Raido** – Raidho, Raitho, Raida, Rad, Reid
6. **Kaunaz** – Kenaz, Kanu, Ken, Kaunan
7. **Gebo** – Gefu, Giba, Gyfu
8. **Wunjo** – Wynja, Wyn, Wunio, Winja
9. **Hagalaz** – Hagal, Hagalas, Hagl, Hagall
10. **Nauthiz** – Nauth, Naud, Naudirz, Nat, Nautiz, Nod, Nied
11. **Isa** – Isa, Eis, Isaz, Isarz, Iss
12. **Jera** – Jer, Jara, Jeran, Jeraz, Gaar
13. **Eihwaz** – Eoh, Eihuaz, Eow, Ihwaz, Iwarz
14. **Pertho** – Perthu, Perth, Peorth, Perthro, Perdhro, Pertra
15. **Algiz** – Eolh, Elhaz, Eoih, Elgr
16. **Sowelo** – Sowulu, Sowilo, Sigel, Sol
17. **Tiwaz** – Tyr, Tiwar, Teiwaz, Tiw, Tew
18. **Berkana** – Berkano, Bairkan, Bjarkan, Beorc, Brica
19. **Eoh** – Ehwaz, Ehwass, Eih, Eh, Exauz, Eyz
20. **Mannaz** – Mann, Madr, Madir, Manna, Mathr
21. **Laguz** – Lagu, Lagus, Lago, Logr, Laaz
22. **Inguz** – Ingwaz, Enguz, Ing
23. **Othila** – Othala, Othilia, Odhil, Othel, Othalan, Odil
24. **Dagaz** – Dags, Daaz, Dag, Deag, Dogr

Heda Church in Sweden was built in the 12th century. It has two rune stones set in the outer walls, both added during the 19th century.

Index

abundance 100–1, 112–13
aetts 27, 64 *see also* Frey's Aett; Hagal's Aett; Tyr's Aett
Ale's stones, Ysad, Sweden 119
Algiz 98–9
Alstad runestone, Norway 178–81
altars 59–60
Ålum runestones, Denmark 164–7
Anglo-Saxon Futhorc 11, 120–1
Anglo-Saxon Rune Poem 121
Ansuz 74–5, 141
Anundshög tumulus, Västmanland, Sweden 130–1
Audhumla 68, 69
aurochs 70–1

bags 27, 59
balance 72–3
Barmen runestone, Norway 170
Berkana 26, 106–7
Bewcastle Cross, England 192–3
bindrunes 141
birch 106–7
birth 106–7
Björketorp runestone, Sweden 144–9
Bluetooth 129
boundaries 72–3
burial chambers 196–201

Caistor-by-Norwich Astragalus 217
casting
    five rune layout 43–5
    layouts overview 37, 56
    magic square layout 54–5
    nine rune layout 49–51
    runic cross layout 52–3
    seven rune layout 46–8
    single rune 38–9
    three rune layout 40–1
    traditional 34–7
cattle 68
celebration 92–3

chance 96–7
change 86–7, 108–9
chaos 86–7
Chessell Down, Isle of Wight, England 214–15
cleansing 59
combination rune readings 34, 51
combs 206–7
commitments 104–5, 108–9
communication 74–5
completion 114–15
cosmology 56
courage 70–1, 104–5

Dagaz 118–19
Dalecarlian runes 123
danegeld 136, 188, 190
danger 90–1
daylight 118–19
Denmark
    inscriptions 206–7
    runestone locations 160–9
destiny 34, 96–7
difficulty 88–9
disruption 86–7
divination *see also* casting
    basic overview 14–16, 27–8
    history 11
    question formulation 28–30
    reading locations 28, 56

Dynna stone, Norway 174–7

Eihwaz 94–5
Einang stone, Norway 170–3
Elder Futhark
    aetts 27, 64, 67 *see also* Frey's Aett; Hagal's Aett; Tyr's Aett
    alternative names 218
    development 11, 64
    name 64
elks 98–9

endings 94–5
England
    inscriptions 202–5, 208–17
    runestone locations 192–3
Englandsstenarna 188
enlightenment 100–1, 118–19
Eoh 108–9

family 114–15, 116–17
fate 34, 96–7
Fehu 34, 64, 68–9, 156
fertility 92–3, 106–7, 114–15
fire 78–9
five rune layout 43–5
flow 112–13
Franks Casket, England 202–5
Frey 67, 114
Frey's Aett 64, 67–82, 122
friendship 110–11
future 28

Gebo 34, 80–1
gemstones 20

gifts 80–1
Greklandsstenarna 188
Grinda, Södermanland, Sweden 188
growth 92–3, 112–13, 118–19

Gunmarp runestone, Sweden 146, 156–7

Hagal 84
Hagalaz 86–7
Hagal's Aett 84, 86–101, 122
hail 86–7
Harald Bluetooth 129, 160
harvest 92–3
healing 98–9, 106–7
health 70–1
Heda runestones, Sweden 219
Heimdall 84
heritage 116–17
home 114–15

hope 118–19
Høre stave church, Norway 182, 184–7
horses 108–9
humanity 110–11
Husby-Sjuhundra church, Uppland, Sweden 188–91

ice 90–1
illumination 100–1, 118–19
Ing 114
Inguz 114–15
inscriptions, history 126–7
interdependence 110–11
intuition 16, 30, 56, 112–13
Isa 90–1
Istaby runestone, Sweden 146, 154–5

Jelling stones, Denmark 160–3
Jera 92–3
jewellery 56–7, 210–11
journeys 76–7
joy 82–3, 92–3, 100–1

Kaunaz 78–9
keystone layout 46–8
knowledge 78–9
Kylver stone, Sweden 140–1

Laguz 112–13
life cycle 94–5
Lilla Vilunda runestones, Sweden 191
Lingsberg runestones, Sweden 132–7
Loveden Hill urn 216, 217
loyalty 108–9

Maeshowe, Orkney, Scotland 196–201
magic square layout 54–5
making rune sets 60–1
mankind 110–11
Mannaz 110–11
materials for rune sets 18–20, 60–1
meditation 27

Mejlby Stone, Denmark 168–9
mindfulness 27
Mjǫllnir 142–3
Möjbro runestone, Sweden 138–9
mythology 11, 22–3, 25, 40, 56

Nauthiz 88–9
needs 88–9
Nerthus 112
Nertus 106
Nikolai Church, Sölvesborg, Sweden 151–3
nine 56
nine rune layout 49–51
Norns 22–3, 25, 40, 56
Norse mythology 11, 22–3, 25, 40, 56
Norway, runestone locations 170–83
numbers, significance of 56

obstacles 90–1
odd numbers 56
Odin 11, 56, 57, 74, 75
Odin's Rune 25, 38
Old English Futhorc 11, 120–1
Orkesta chirch, Uppland, Sweden 190
Orkney Islands 196–201
Othila 116–17

pawn 96–7
pendants 210–11
pentagrams 150
Pertho 96–7
positivity 30
pouches 59
power 100–1
protection 94–5, 98–9

quartz 59
question formulation 28–30

Raido 34, 76–7
reading runes 30–4 *see also* divination

Ribe comb 206
Rök runestone, Östergötland, Sweden 7, 126, 129, 158–9
Roskitil runic cross, Kirk Braddan, Isle of Man 10
rune cloths 28, 34, 56
rune sets, choosing 18–24
rune symbols, learning 25–7
runes
    first recorded use of word 170
    origins 10–11
    uses 11, 14–17
runestones, location and history overview 126–7 *see also specific*

countries
runic cross layout 52–3
runic V layout 46–8
Ruthwell Cross, Scotland 194–5

Scandinavian Futhark 11, 122
Scotland, runes locations 194–201
Seax of Beagnoth 208–9
self-care 99, 107, 110–11
seven rune layout 46–8
Sigurd carving, Lake Malaren, Sweden 132–3
Skuld 40, 41
Sowelo 100–1
stave churches 182–3, 184–7
Stenfoten runestone, Sweden 146, 150–1
Stenkvista runestone, Sweden 142–3
storage 59
strength 70–1, 104–5, 118–19
success 100–1
sun 100–1
Sunna 100
Sweden, runestone locations 7, 119, 126, 128–59, 188–91, 219
sword mounts/sheaths/scabbards 212–15
swords 208–9
symbol-side down readings 30–1

symbol upside down readings 31

Tacitus 11, 34, 36
talismans 17, 56–8
Thames Scramasax 208–9
Thor 72–3

thorns 72
Thor's hammer 142
three 56
three rune layout 40–1
Thurisaz 72–3
Tiwaz 104–5, 141
Tolkien, J. R. R. 14
torch 78–9
town runes 182–3
'training sticks' 103, 129, 182–3
travel 76–7, 108–9
Tree of Life 56, 94–5
trust 108–9
Tyr 102, 104–5
Tyr's Aett 102, 104–19, 122

Undley Bracteate 210–11
Urd 40
urns 216, 217
Uruz 70–1

Väsby runestones, Sweden 190
Verdandi 40–1
Vimose, Denmark 206–7

water 112–13
wealth 68–9
willpower 98–9
writing 16–17
Wunjo 34, 82–3
Wyrd stone 25, 34, 64

year 92–3
yew 94–5
Yggdrasil 56, 94–5
Younger Futhark 11, 122–3

Picture Credits

Alamy: 73 (Album), 81 (Lebrecht Music & Arts), 83 (Heritage Image Partnership), 89 (Lebrecht Music & Arts), 93 (Stig Alenas), 95 (Scott Flaherty), 103 (Colin Waters), 109 (AF Fotografie), 115 (Janzig/Europe), 119 (Joachim Hofmann), 135 & 137 (Michal Sikorski), 148/149 (Leslie Garland Pictures), 176/177 (Prisma Archivo), 186/187 (Jorge Tutor), 195 (Hugh McKean), 198/199 (Homer Sykes), 211 (World History Archive)

Mark Batley: 157

Dreamstime: 12/13 (Pasiphae), 14 (Werasen), 15 (Ronin69), 25 (franbart462), 29 (Starblue), 31 (Lightpro), 41 (Ivashkova), 42 (Volha Yarmolenka), 44 (Filindmitriy86), 62 (PhotoChur), 65 & 85 (Pelaroja), 87 (Omyim1637), 91 (Jamenpercy), 99 (Jocrebbin), 107 (Arcticphotoworks), 111 (Allexxe), 113 (Fyletto), 126 (Pyroe79), 129 (Svetlana Serdiukova), 132/133 (Pinkbadger), 152/153 (Rui Baiao) 159 (Ellah), 161 (Natagolubnycha), 163 (Fotoember), 184/185 (Rpbmedia), 219 (Thomasmales)

Getty Images: 10 (Print Collector), 61 (Olena Ruban), 69 (Pictures From History/Universal Images Group), 71 (Godong/Universal Images Group), 75 (Pictures From History/Universal Images Group), 77 (De Agostini), 79 (Universal Images Group), 97 (Roberto Machado Noa), 101 (Universal Images Group), 105 (Pictures from History), 117 (Heritage Images), 124/125 (Culture Club), 180/181 (Universal Images Group), 204/205 (Print Collector)

GNU Free Documentation Licence: 143 (Berig), 165 & 167 (Calvin), 189 & 191 (Berig)

Licensed under the Creative Commons Attribution 2.5 Generic Licence: 155 (Bengdt A Lundberg), 171 (John Erling Blad)

Licensed under the Creative Commons Attribution-Share Alike 2.0 Generic Licence: 139 (Marieke Kuijjer)

Licensed under the Creative Commons Attribution-Share Alike 3.0 Unported Licence: 141 (Gunnar Creutz), 151 (Sendelbach), 169 (Nationalmuseet), 193 (Doug Sim), 207 (Nationalmuseet), 208/209 (BabelStone)

Licensed under the Creative Commons Attribution-Share Alike 4.0 Licence: 7 (Arkland)

Licensed under the Creative Commons Attribution-Share Alike 4.0 International Licence: 172/173 (Lars Gustavsen)

Public Domain: 22/23, 57, 120, 123

Shutterstock: 8 (Neirfy), 16 (Ira Sokolovskaya), 17 (Artha Design Studio), 18 (PhotoChur), 19 (Ekaterina Vidiasova), 20 (beingeniusloci), 21 (Stock1537), 24 (Plateresca), 26 (Volha Werasen), 32/33 (Adria Black), 35 (FotoHelin), 36 (Renata Sedmakova), 48 (Sutterstock AI), 51 (Shaiith), 58 (Dirceu Jose de Santana), 66 (Anna Torba), 130/131 (Ingrid Pakats), 145, 147 (Imfoto), 200/201 (Pecold)

Shutterstock/Smeilov Sergey: 38, 39, 40, 45, 46, 50, 53, 55

The Trustees of the British Museum: 212/213, 215, 217

All images of the runic alphabet for chapter two are by Anielius via Shutterstock

Background illustrations are by Bourbon-88 via Shutterstock and Arkadii Ivanchenko, Viktor Kostenko via Dreamstime